Shulamis

Stories from a Montreal Childhood

Shulamis

Stories from a Montreal Childhood

Shulamis Yelin

Shoreline

SHULAMIS
Stories from a Montreal Childhood

© Shulamis Yelin 1993

Printed in Canada by: Les Ateliers Graphiques Marc Veilleux Inc.
Cap-Saint-Ignace, Quebec

Published by: Shoreline
23 Ste-Anne, Ste-Anne-de-Bellevue, Quebec, H9X 1L1
(514) 457-5733   SAN: 1169564

Photographs: Notman Photograhic Archives of the McCord Museum of Canadian History; personal collection of Shulamis Yelin.

Some of these stories have appeared in The Reconstructionist Magazine, Pioneer Women Magazine, The Canadian Zionist, B'nai B'rith Monthly (Geneva) and The Canadian Jewish Anthology.

First published by Vehicule Press 1983, with two reprintings in 1984.

Depot legal 1993: Bibliotheque nationale du Quebec,
and National Library of Canada

CANADIAN CATALOGUING IN PUBLICATION DATA

Yelin, Shulamis, 1913-
    Shulamis: stories from a Montreal childhood

ISBN 0-9695180-7-2

1. Yelin, Shulamis, 1913-   . 2. Montreal (Quebec) -- Biography.
3. Jews -- Quebec (Province) -- Montreal -- Biography. I. Title.

FC2947.26.Y44A3 1993 971.4' 2800492402 C93-090628-4
F1054.5.M853Y45 1993

For Papa -- who set the tone

*For Mamma --
who supplied the lyrics*

*for my little sister Denie --
who said that
tho' she sang off key
it sounded lovely
inside*

*and for my Bubbie
who stands before me --
an open door
the fragrance of her memory
inviting me in.*

Contents

Preface 11
Purim 15
Early Sorrow 18
Enter Denie -- The New Baby 22
Scarlet Fever 25
My Zaida, the *Kohen*, the Carpenter 29
I Find My Jewish Name 34
Papa Finds a Country 38
Winnie 42
Denie Prepares for School 46
I Unroll Denie in School 50
I Learn the Facts of Life 55
Denie Learns Sewing 60
Shekspir was Jewis 64
Denie Needs a Tonic 69
For the Love of a Kid 72
Sweet Corn and Bringing Up Children 78
I Take Scripture 99
The Girl Who Stole Santa Claus 103
Highland Fling 111
The Joys of Winter 119
Dora 124
Reading 128
True Romances 133
My First Party 137
The Four Doors 142
Transitions 147
Kasha and Loving Kindness 152
Leaving Home 155
I Become a Teacher 158
Encounters 161
Rite of Passage 163
Afterword -- About the Author 170
Photographs 81-96

Foreword to the Fourth Edition of Shulamis: Stories from a Montreal Childhood

A Fourth Edition! A Tenth Anniversary! Little did I think when I took that taxi ride down to de Bullion and Prince Arthur Streets on Montreal's east side in the springtime of 1963, that I was embarking on a book of memoirs about my childhood. All I was looking for was reflections on the early years, those pre-adolescent years when I attended the afternoon classes of the Jewish Peretz Shule. I had been asked to write a short memoir to draw attention to the forthcoming Fiftieth Anniversary of the school's existence.

When the piece appeared in the local Jewish news I was bombarded with compliments.

"It's wonderful!"
"You brought back so many memories!"
"You must tell more stories about that time."

And so over the years, memories arose -- memories not only related to the schule, but to my Yiddish speaking home and family, to Colonial Avenue near Prince Arthur (the street on which we lived), and to the English Protestant Strathearn School which entered me into a second culture. And stories were born which finally became the book whose Fourth Edition we are celebrating today.

At the same time, we celebrate the Tenth Anniversary of *Shulamis'* continued popularity. Copies of *Shulamis* are found as bedside books, as gifts, and in schools and colleges for Literature, Social Studies, History, Creative Writing and simple entertainment -- filled with stories which evoke memories in others who may continue to enrich our literature with tales of their own remembering.

Mention must be made of Vehicule Press which issued and reissued the first beautiful edition three times in eight months to keep up with the demand. Requests came from as far as Reikjavik, Iceland; Duisberg, West Germany; Paris, France; and Yellowknife, NWT; to say nothing of requests from across Canada and the United States.

My special thanks must go Judy Mappin of the Double Hook Book Store, who, knowing that the book was completely sold out, approached Judy Isherwood of Shoreline Press to republish it. Mrs. Mappin felt, as did a number of librarians, that the book is a classic and should not be allowed to remain out of print. I must heartily commend Mrs. Isherwood on her alacrity and zeal in getting the book out at this time.

While the stories in the book remain the same, a new cover and several new pictures mark the Fourth Edition and the Tenth Anniversary of *Shulamis: Stories from a Montreal Childhood*.

I pray that future readers will reap as much pleasure from this edition as others who have read it in the past.

Shulamis Yelin
November 1, 1993

Preface

In 1963, when the Jewish Peretz School celebrated its fiftieth anniversary, a strange yearning awoke in me to return to the old street in that one-time Jewish neighbourhood. It was at least twenty years since I had last visited the area.

The Peretz School -- the Shule -- is a vivid part of my childhood memory. Not the bright new Shule on Cote St. Luc with its broad halls, floors and neon-lighted days; not the many rented flats where children spent the dimly lit after-school hours seeking to tie the elusive knots which bound them to their ancient many-storied past; not even the renovated building (formerly a factory) on Duluth Street where I taught in the first Dayschool Kindergarten to open its doors gratis to children of survivors of the Holocaust.

My Shule was in the great old house on Cadieux Street (now de Bullion) above Prince Arthur, across from the iron-fenced stone nunnery with its tall trees and mystery-shrouded dormer windows a hundred or more yards from the Jewish Maternity Hospital from which weird wailings could be heard in my Bubbie's house next door. Flanked by the red brick walls of neighbouring houses, the school stood in modest retirement off the busy street. Its large bay windows, like heavy-lidded eyes, bore witness to the changing tempo, changing times. Its gray slotted box-benches concealed untold childhood treasures: a well-sharpened pencil slipped from the hands of a child completing his homework or resting from his games; a large copper penny with a portrait of King George; a tiny silver five cent piece -- today a collector's item. The large earthen courtyard harboured a lone elm with patches of grass trying valiantly to grow around it despite the constant traffic of children's feet. The well-worn winding stairs within were alive, singing their many-voiced descants to the psalms of our youthful ascents and descents.

That was a long time ago.

The sun is bright and a premature spring wind riffles the puddles which steal their way into the gaps in the snow. I hail a cab and ask to be released at the corner of the street where I had lived.

As I walk up Colonial Avenue I seem to feel a previous incarnation. The house we lived in with its winding iron staircase still stands. It looks loved and cared for with its coat of fresh paint and cheerful curtains. On these stairs I had skidded on a cold winter's day when, in fantasy of being a beautiful famous actress, I had let go of the banister and had hit bottom on my dignity. Here, on the other side of the lane where we had skipped and played marbles, stands the old Malo house where, after Mr. Malo's death, little bleeding hearts had blown in the tiny garden every summer. Now the outer wooden doors had been removed.

On all sides memories jostle each other as I look about, recalling moments, people, dreams. The only false note comes from the new-fangled street lamp which replaces the one I recall, the one that stood right across from our parlour window casting in the night an intricate pattern through the lace curtains of our triptych bay window onto the carpeted floor.

I mustn't stop. There, across the road is the high wooden fence with the latched door through which I used to find my way up the back stairs into the school on Cadieux Street. Yet, as I look, the building seems to have vanished. The fence is there but I find no sign of the building above it.

I move quickly down Prince Arthur Street. It is quite as it was. The names on the shops are different but the buildings are the same. On the left is Choquette's candy store -- still a candy store, but no longer owned by the angry moustached little Frenchman who hated children yet sold only candy and tobacco. Beside it is the Chinese laundry. Is this the laundry man who gave me lychee nuts when I came for our package and a glorious many-coloured glass bangle at Christmas?

Our neighbour, Malo's stately candy shop, still stands diagonally opposite Dover's Grocery, but here the decorous wooden doors have been removed and a shabby glass business window announces some textile firm.

Quickly I hurry up the street. How many times have I hurried up this same street in fear of being late, in fear of missing something at the Shule.

Yet I seem to be taking too many steps. Between the two tall red brick walls which seem to have grown so strangely close together, the courtyard where we played has become a brown muddy square deeply gouged with the massive tires of freight trucks. Three men are loading merchandise into one of these trucks. But where is the Shule? There in the background beyond the walls, stands an old brown longhouse.

Surely there is some mistake. I probably haven't gone far enough up the street. I must look a little further.

But no. I recognize my Bubbie's house and beside it the large glass-windowed doors with the Mogen Davids, the windows of the sadly neglected Jewish Maternity Hospital. It is now a private dwelling with several shabby-looking children sitting on the steps.

How it has all changed since my early remembering! Gone are the long slotted benches upon which we had sat. There is not even a vestige of the chalk marks of our childhood on the recently repainted red brick walls. The Shule, like a shrunken aging giant stares somberly at me across the empty courtyard.

There is a sense of loss in me -- a sense of bereavement.

I look with suspended breath across the street for that other landmark, the nunnery with its beautiful garden. The gray building stands denuded, stripped of its trees and bushes -- it is now a factory. The "dismounting stone" in front of its gate is gone; in an earlier day gracious ladies had used it to step from their horse-drawn carriages to the sidewalk.

An era has passed away.

Purim

The first three years of my life were spent in the home of my Bubbie (grandmother) and my Zaida (grandfather), and all my links with holiday and festival stem from their home.

A great rocking chair smiles at me out of the distant past.

My Zaida, the carpenter, had built that rocking chair. It was not just a straight-backed rocker with two straight arms to hold onto as you rocked to and fro, but a great half-moon of a vehicle with huge upside-down rainbows that sped back and forth on a journey to nowhere -- a rocker that knew all the tests and tempers of childhood and all the impediments of growing old.

When I got to know it, the rocker was already brown with age and use and was still the favourite means of conveyance to the heights of childhood ecstasy and to the haven of peace which is the dream of the heavy-hearted.

One gray March morning before the festival of Purim, I sat tailor-fashion in the rocker in a corner of the kitchen, singing a folk rhyme my Zaida had taught me, the rhyme of the Purim masqueraders as they went trick-or-treating from door to door.

> Haynt is Purim
> Morgn is ois
> Gib mir a groshn
> Un varf mich arois.

> Today is Purim
> Tomorrow it's o'er
> Give me a penny
> And show me the door.

I could see my Bubbie scraping from the great earthenware bowl the pastry dough for the plump poppy-seed hamantashen and taiglach she was making. I could feel the wave of warmth coming towards me from the oven and could smell the crackling firewood and the brown molten honey in which the taiglach would be cooked.

Through the doorway of the adjoining dining room I could see my Zaida at his morning devotions. His face was turned to the eastern wall, a reminder that his heart lay in the East, in Jerusalem, where the western wall of King Solomon's great temple still stood. As he finished his prayers, he stood watching me rock as he unwound his phylacteries and folded up his great prayer shawl. His dark eyes shone but his face was pale and drawn beneath his gray pointed beard, for he had just come through one of his frequent bouts of asthma.

"Why don't you sing a Purim song?" he suggested. "Tomorrow we will go to the Synagogue to read the Megillah of Esther. You must be ready for Purim so you can boo Haman when his name is read."

Boo Haman! I recalled the joyous celebration of the year before -- the synagogue warm and glowing, bulging with young and old, and the voices of all commingling as the Rabbi chanted from the scroll the story of the beautiful Queen Esther who, on the advice of her Uncle Mordecai, had braved the presence of the Persian King Ahasuerus, and had prevailed upon him to save her people from the horrendous decree of the villainous Haman. And every time his abhorrent name was mentioned, it was followed by an extended roll of wooden noise-makers, graggers, and the curse, Yemach Shemoh! (May his name be wiped out.) Thus had Jews revelled in the miracles of their survival throughout their long and painful history.

"Come, Zaida," I called. "Come rock with me!"

Soon he was beside me.

"Sit on the arm of the chair," he suggested, putting his arm around me as he sat down, "and we'll sing together."

What joy it was for me as he began to sing in his sweet husky voice the traditional Purim canticle, Shoshanus Yaakov.

> How the roses of Jacob
> watched with joy and glory
> as Mordecai rode through the streets
> robed in Royal Purple!

For me, the room was filled with the scent of roses.

"Baruch," begged my Bubbie, "go and eat. You haven't had a thing to eat yet. Upon my word, he has the soul of a child; the rocking chair and Shoshanus Yaakov are on his mind, and he just out of a sick bed!"

"All the more reason to be grateful and to remember God's miracles," replied my Zaida.

Our voices filled the room. As the chair went faster and faster, Mordecai and Esther stood before me dancing a courtly dance to the rhythm of the music. Ahasuerus, in all his splendour, applauded as he watched them, and Haman, Yimach Shemo, hung his head in shame as Ahasuerus' horse tried to gallop to our beat.

Mordecai looked like my Zaida, and strangely enough, Esther looked like the picture of my Bubbie. Even the rocking chair had a face -- the face of Ahasuerus' smiling horse.

Early Sorrow

It was in the downstairs flat on Colonial Avenue above Rachel Street that I first knew the pain of separation. Out of its large glass front-parlour window, I could see the tall tree with its sparsely-leafed branches of early spring, but I recall no sunshine in that room. I recall only a gray morning mist through which a little girl of three, with blond bottle curls, properly dressed as always, moved silently, holding a large round silver balloon on a stick, marching round and round in a parade of her own.

That was the spring we moved out of my Bubbie's house to a place of our own.

Suddenly it was quiet. No longer was there the chorus of voices of the young aunts and uncles returning from work or school, no longer was there the rustle of my Bubbie's quick-moving long white apron or the rattle of the large pots and pans on the woodstove in the basement kitchen as she prepared the meals and baked the bread for the large busy family. We were alone in our own flat, Papa, Mamma and I. Mamma in the kitchen, Papa at work, and I -- at the large window looking out.

At night we were together in the back parlour which served as the family bedroom. Papa and Mamma in the big bed in the middle of the room, I in my small bed in the corner to the right.

I felt even lonelier at night.

"Why can't I sleep with you and Papa?" I begged.

"You're a big girl now," said Mamma. "You're three years old. We have our own house and you have your own bed because you are a big girl."

I did not feel very big. I felt very lonely. I missed the large family of aunts and uncles who scolded and fussed over me. I missed the embracing warmth of that big house.

The only one I did not miss was the Auntie Faygl. She was dark and squat and always dressed in black. Her eyes were eternally angry and she never opened her mouth without issuing what I heard as a snarl. Even her laughter was a yelp. She was childless and liked to pinch me with the stubby fingers of her short stout hand. I was afraid of her and ran to hide behind Mamma whenever she was there.

On Saturday nights, when the family gathered around my Bubbie's great dining-room table, Auntie Faygl refused to sit down. She stood behind my Zaida's chair under the big wooden clock with the brown horse ornament. She neither spoke nor ate -- the skeleton at the feast.

In the new house she began to appear to me in a recurring nightmare.

I awoke screaming, "Mamma! Mamma!"

"What is it?" Mamma asked in a distant voice.

"Mamma! Mamma!" I screamed again.

In the dream she was standing in her accustomed place behind Zaida's chair under the clock. The family was enjoying the feast Bubbie had set before them, but Auntie Faygl was not part of the celebration. She was glowering at me as she wound the clock. Suddenly she pointed at me with her yellow fingernail.

"Mamma!"

"She's dreaming," said Papa, turning on the light.

He picked me up and sat me on his lap at the edge of their bed.

"It's Auntie Faygl!" I sobbed shrilly, clinging to him in terror. "With the horse."

"It's only a dream," said Papa, rocking me gently. "Only a dream. What is the Auntie doing?"

"She's winding up the big clock in Bubbie's dining room! And the clock is screaming and the horsie is jumping on me!"

I trembled as I related the horror of my nightmare.

"It's nothing," Mamma comforted, coming close to us. "See? Nobody is here, just Papa and you and me ...."

"You had a bad dream," Papa repeated. "That horsie on the clock is a toy horse. He can't hurt you ...."

"But the Auntie Faygl," I cried.

"She isn't even here. See? It's just a bad dream," Mamma repeated.

"Wait, I'll get you a glass of water so it'll go away," Papa offered, returning me to my own bed.

The nightmare occurred again and again and in my own small bed I felt lonelier than ever.

One Sunday morning, Mamma dressed me early in a white silky dress she had sewn for me, a dress which I clearly recall had little pink flowers scattered over it, a dress with a small frill at the hem and neckline. As she combed my hair into curls and tied them to one side with a pink ribbon, she said, "Today we are going to Dominion Park. We will have lots of fun there."

It was a long ride by tram to the amusement park. Papa carried me on and off the car in his arms, and out of the distant past, I recall my first sight of that magical country with the huge Ferris wheel -- its little red flags moving round and round, its metal baskets cradling its squealing passengers high above the crowd.

A greater wonder was soon to appear before me. I dragged Papa to see where the music was pulling me, the music of the calliope which played for the galloping ponies of the merry-go-round.

What beautiful ponies! Painted ponies with trappings in crimson, silver, and gold! I must ride one of them -- that white one with the crimson bridle and the golden mane!

As we waited for the ride to come to an end, Papa bought me a ticket and soon I was ensconced on the white wooden pony of my choice, clinging to his golden mane, terrified yet elated. The music started up again and we were away. Up and down and round and round to the music of the calliope we went, on an unreal pony to the real world of childhood. The screams which were first heard as the music started again subsided with our rising joy.

It was hard to pry me off that pony. It was only the bribe of that silver balloon that got me off.

☆ ☆ ☆

I was up early the next morning, eyeing my silver balloon as it stood bobbing gently in the corner of my bed on its tall thin stick. How I had prized and fondled it until bedtime! It was the symbol of all my pleasure of my day at the fair, the day which for a time, had wiped out that loneliness which had enwrapped me.

I don't know what I actually wore that morning. I recall myself only in that silky dress, the little girl with the blond curls and sad face, holding my balloon upright in my left hand, marching round and round in the front parlour under the high ceiling, humming my own little tune in imitation of the calliope, riding my imaginary gold-maned pony, watching my reflection in the tall floor mirror which stood in the corner by the window.

Mamma looked in for a moment, smiled, and walked away.

The room was warm and I continued on my imaginary ride, alone, with the remembered troupe of ponies following my lead, the sound of the calliope echoing in my ears.

Suddenly there was a loud bang. I shrieked. Mamma came running. I was crying wildly.

My balloon had burst in the warm air near the ceiling. It hung in silver tatters.

Enter Denie -- The New Baby

Soon Mamma began to spend her mornings in bed. Papa served me my breakfast and I played quietly in the front parlour while Mamma rested. Later she would rise to fix our lunch and then Mamma and I would go for a short walk. Often we stopped at the shop windows to admire their wares.

As time wore on, Mamma began to stop at the Main Furniture Store. "See that nice baby carriage?" she would ask. "Like for a doll but bigger. For a real baby." I nodded my approval and we walked on.

I was glad to be spending so much time with Mamma. I was beginning to accept the new house and the conditions of aloneness in the family. Over and over again Mamma told me I was a Big Girl, not a baby like my auntie's baby who still suckled at the breast. I could feed myself and could even dress myself, except for tying the laces of my tall shoes. I could play by myself for hours with the toys Papa brought home and not trouble Mamma who was delicate and who needed much rest.

Early one morning in May, Papa woke me.

"You must get dressed quickly," he said. "I will take you to Bubbie's house."

As he helped me into my clothes, I could hear Mamma moan.

"Mamma?" I queried tremulously.

"Go with Papa, Sophela," she said softly. "I'll see you later."

When Papa brought me home again in the later afternoon, Mamma was still in bed. She lay propped up on the big thick feather pillows which had been part of her dowry. A fresh white counterpane covered the bed. Her face was pale and her thick auburn hair was loosely plaited in a crown on her head. The room had a sweetish smell of disinfectant.

Auntie greeted me at the door.

"Come and see the new baby," she said. "See how pretty she is."

"Baby?" I looked about the room but could see nothing.

"Come here, by the bed, Sophela," Mamma invited softly.

I ran to Mamma.

"Not too close," cautioned Auntie, lifting me so I could see.

"See how small she is. Sleeping right there in your Mamma's arm."

Timidly I glanced at the mystery called "baby". There she lay, a tiny red face with a fringe of orange hair. The eyes were shut and the tiny bud of a mouth was busy making sucking noises.

"This is your little sister Denie," Mamma introduced us, exposing the infant's hand.

But even as I marveled at the diminutive wonder, I withdrew instinctively from the rival who was claiming Mamma's attention.

"She's your little sister," Mamma repeated. "See her tiny fingers? See her tiny nose?"

All I could see was Mamma's love for the stranger who lay in her bed, in the place where I wanted to be but was not allowed.

A few days later I stood by the large front parlour window looking out while Mamma sat in her rocker nursing the baby. Suddenly a large horse-drawn wagon drew up before our house. A huge man descended and pulled out two large bulky packages wrapped in straw and brown paper.

Auntie, who had again dropped in to visit, let him in.

"Vichna, the furniture is here," she announced.

I looked on as the man unwrapped the cradle and the carriage we had seen in the store window. No, those things weren't for me. They were for the New Baby.

The following Sunday, as Mamma moved slowly about the house, she said, "Today we are having a party. All the aunties are coming and we will throw candy into the baby's cradle and into her carriage so she will have a sweet life."

We stood by the cradle on the left side of the big bed. The cradle was all white except for the red ribbons Mamma had tied on it to ward off the evil eye. There lay the baby dressed in the long cotton dimity dress Mamma had prepared in advance, a dress with dozens of tiny tucks alternating with narrow bands of fine lace and white ribbon. Mamma opened a large paper bag of sugar-dipped orange marmalade candies and said with a fond smile to the aunts and Papa and me, "Here, take. Throw in the cradle. Our Denie should have a sweet life."

"A sweet life! A sweet life!" they echoed, carefully throwing the candy near the baby's feet.

"Now in the carriage," Papa urged, and the ceremony was repeated with the same words, "A sweet life! A sweet life!"

Only I remained distant and silent.

If your sweet tooth says **Candy**
Your wisdom tooth will say
Buy GRANDMOTHERS

Posen's Photo Studio

are now at

78-80 FAIRMOUNT W.

for appointment telephone
BE lair 0097

and

3711 St. Lawrence Blvd.
Tel. PLateau 7539

POSEN'S PHOTO STUDIO
well known Montreal Photographer

LAncaster 7050

B. MALCOFF
TAILOR FOR YOUNG MEN

Suits and Overcoats Made-to-Order.
We also have a fine assortment of
Spring O'Coats, Ready-to-Wear
Made in our own shop

3483 ST. LAWRENCE BLVD.

פראפ. יעקב ראזמארין

(מוזיק דירעקטאר און לערער פון דער פרץ שולע)

גיט לעקציעס אין פיאנא, טעאריע און הארמאניע

85 מאונט ראיאל וועסט
אפארט. 3

טעלעפאן. בעלעיר 3667-דזשיי

Marcus
LUNCH & DELICATESSEN

וילט איר האבען א גוטן מאלצייט
א סטייק אדער גוטע געשמאקע סענדוויטשעס

ראן קומט צו

1449 סט. לארענס בולוואר
טעל. פלאצא 2914.

A page of advertisements from Yiddishe Kinder, the magazine published on the occasion of the 7th graduation of the Peretz Shule, May 1927.

Scarlet Fever

The only time I recall sitting on Mamma's knees was when I had scarlet fever.

I was four and a half years old. I was wearing a white flannel nightdress with pink ribbon running through a band of eyelet embroidery about the neck and wrists. My tow-coloured hair was in curls and I felt very warm. I clung to Mamma as we sat by the parlour window in the late afternoon, the white lace curtain drawn aside. We were facing our family doctor as he drew the neckband of my nightgown down, examined my chest, and applied the stethoscope.

Our doctor was a gentle man, smaller than Papa. I recall him, in the afternoon grayness, a brown presence: his suit was brown, his tie was brown, the little buttons on his vest were brown, his short hair was brown as was his small closely-cropped moustache. Even his voice, which was somewhat high-pitched, had a soft, brown quality that seemed both odd and comforting to me.

As he folded away his stethoscope, he looked first to Mamma and then to me and said gently, "Sophie would you like to go to the hospital?"

I clutched at Mamma's housedress, pressing my head against her breast. I didn't know what the word "hospital" meant, but I did know that I didn't want to go anywhere. I wanted to stay right where I was, on Mamma's lap, in our parlour by the window.

"With scarlet fever you have to go to the hospital," he explained.

I began to cry. I seemed to sense some scheme to separate me from this finally familiar place.

"Don't cry," he comforted me, trying to take my hand, which I drew away. "You will be with lots of other children. They, too, have to leave their Mamma for a little while."

I looked at Mamma through tears. Was she willing to let me go? I looked to the crib in the corner of the other half of the double parlour where we all slept, and I trembled.

Was it because of the New Baby that I had to be sent away?

As if in answer to my unasked question, our doctor said, "You don't want the Baby to get sick too, do you?"

What had my being sick to do with the New Baby? Ever since she had come into our house I was reminded to step down and make room for That Baby! I cried even more profusely.

"Your Mamma will buy you a nice big doll, won't you, Mamma?" the doctor cued her in.

I had never had a real doll. I had lots of toys: a small table and a rocking chair, a large spinning top that hummed as it rotated, a painted wooden Russian doll-within-a-doll-within-a-doll-within-a-doll, a round-bottomed Santa that rocked and rocked and didn't fall over -- and there were many more small ones that the New Baby had broken. But a doll? Mamma always made one for me from a towel, nice and cuddly. That was my doll.

I pointed to my doll in the shoe-box by the wall.

"Do you want a real doll?" he asked again.

For the moment I was distracted. "Yes," I answered, drying my eyes with my knuckles.

"Good," said the doctor and, turning to Mamma, he said, "Don't worry, Mrs. Borodensky. She'll be all right there. It's better for her in the hospital. You can't keep her at home."

I recall a strange husky man and a large red woolen blanket. I began to cry loudly as Mamma stepped away from my bed to let him wrap me and take me away.

The rest comes back in the light of a nightmare -- Papa and Mamma were standing by the open doors of the long black ambulance while the man strapped me to the stretcher inside. No words were spoken, no one was crying. Even I was not crying. I was two children -- I was the observer intrigued by the ongoing ceremony, and I was the victim, anguished by my expulsion from our home.

As the heavy doors closed, leaving me in near darkness, I cried again. Was it right that I should be ejected from that house because of the New Baby, should leave my place and familiar things to her, and without a word or sound accept this exile to an unknown place via that long black wagon?

Turning my head, I saw beside me the large head of a lifeless doll. I knew I wouldn't love her. Despite her dark eyes and black hair, I saw her as that pink and white red-headed Baby who slept in the crib on the other side of the big bed, in the back parlour, that Baby who had made me again a stranger.

What happened to the doll? I don't recall ever seeing her again. Did I reject her after that first night or did she become part of the communal toy chest in the children's ward of St. Paul's Hospital for Communicable Diseases? I don't know, and in the totally new surroundings, I don't recall ever longing for her or remembering her with love.

I can still feel the dark red aura of the ward. Perhaps it was the fever that gripped me or the reflection of my red spots on the dark woolen blankets. What I remember best is the two long lines of small white iron cots, each with a wooden chair beside it and the mysterious floating motion of the black-garbed, hooded nuns with their white coifs who tended to us.

I recall the first morning I was allowed off the bed to wash myself: the small stepladder I had to mount to reach the sink, the brushing of my teeth with the Forhan's toothpaste Mamma had provided, and the sweet-tasting Dobell's tablet in a gargle we were encouraged to use each day.

I recall kneeling in prayer at the nun's feet to repeat words in a language I did not understand, the smiling face of the little Sister who taught me how to roll my hair ribbons on the lower wooden rung of the chair so they would be straight and ready for wear again the next day.

I recall the admonitions of the nuns as they hurried us into bed and put out all the lights except the small night light at the end of the hall. "Vatkooshay perkon veezeet," ("Va te coucher parce qu'on visite") we repeated laughing as we hurried into bed. What it meant I didn't know, but it sounded auspicious.

I recall, too, the Bigger Boy in the running shoes who plagued me when I was lonely, who said that my brown wrapper and carpet slippers were bought from a rag peddler, and although I knew he was wrong, yet, might he not be right? For what could one expect from a mother who stood quietly by as they took her child in a huge red blanket and tied her onto a board with wide straps in a black wagon which took her from her own bed, her home and all that was familiar?

I never grew accustomed to the ward. A small brown wrapper-clad child with ribbon-plaited hair, I walked sadly between the rows of beds in my carpet slippers, humming little tunes to myself.

The days that Mamma came to visit were the hardest. Did other parents come too? I don't know. I only know I was invited to come to the window, and there below, just off the green lawn with its bright geranium beds, stood Mamma in her dark skirt and white silk blouse, smiling and waving to me. I felt nothing. Once my Bubbie stood with her, my Bubbie in her black Sabbath dress and peruke. She didn't smile. Her white hands were folded and as she looked at me I felt a rush of love.

Later the little Sister unwrapped a package by my bed.

"Your Mamma asked if she could bring something. We told her to bring a Bible with your name in it so we could pray for you." I could picture my Bubbie at her Sabbath candles, covering her eyes as she prayed.

✡ ✡ ✡

Why can't I recall the moment when I was told I would be going home? Surely that must have evoked some feeling in me. I recall sitting on top of the small ladder in the ward washroom as the little Sister dressed me and combed out my hair. A small smile passed between us. She was my friend. As she pulled the freshly unrolled ribbon through my hair, tugging it to and fro to get it just right, I felt another tug -- a movement within me, tugging me to and fro ....

Mamma met me downstairs. She smiled and took my hand and we walked out onto the pavement between the lawns and the flower beds to go home. Because it was Saturday, Papa could not come. It was his busiest day at the store.

On Sunday afternoon, the young aunts and uncles came to celebrate my homecoming. There were presents and smiles and we all had tea. I sat with them all at the table, silent, my inward eye at the hospital. I could not help wondering what the little Sister and the Bigger Boy were doing then.

My Zaida the *Kohen*, the Carpenter

My Zaida was a carpenter. He was also a kohen.

My Zaida had a special place in the Shomrim Laboker (Watchers of the Morning) Synagogue. He was the eldest kohen and, as my Bubbie said, "next to the Cantor" he had the sweetest voice.

To be a kohen today doesn't mean very much to most Jews. Many do not even carry the name, and to many who do, it means only that their name is Cohn, Cohen, Kahane, Cowan, or some similar sounding surname. Many kohanim by birth (an honour passed on from either parent to children), do not even bear the name, having it changed through marriage or other circumstance. To some it means only that they may not enter a room where there is a dead body. The proscription remains despite the passing of the rites of the kohanim which forbade them to be near anything "unclean."

My Zaida's name was not Kohen. He stemmed from a family of dayan-im, rabbinical judges. When Alexander the Second of Russia decreed that Jews adopt surnames, Zaida's grandfather had assumed the name of Bar-dayan-sky, son of a dayan; this came to be written Bardiansky on my grandfather's passport. In time, each son sought his own individuality, and the family found its name in the telephone book under the various spellings of Bordensky, Borodensky, Bordansky, Bordan, and Borden.

My Zaida never forgot he was a kohen, and to him and his friends at the synagogue this implied chosenness.

"The kohanim in the Temple were the leaders, the special servants of God," he told us. "Dressed in white, they offered up the sacrifices, performed the necessary services and blessed the people. The people loved and respected them.

"Most important of all was the High Priest, the Kohen Godol. Like Moses' brother Aaron or like Mattathias of the Chanukah story, only he was permitted to enter the Holy of Holies, the place where the Holy Spirit dwelt."

When I remembered that my Zaida was the eldest kohen in his synagogue, I thought of him as the Kohen Godol. As I watched him at prayer in his fine woolen prayer shawl with the broad black bands and the long knotted fringes, his face framed in its silver embroidered neck band, I knew he was special just like the High Priest, Mattathias.

When he raised his voice in the age-old cantillations of our people, he was still my Zaida, but I had become the granddaughter of the Kohen Godol of Modin, or perhaps even of King Solomon's Temple.

The members of the Shomrim Laboker Synagogue had made an all-important decision. They had decided to build a new building. The work went ahead very rapidly -- it must be ready for the High Holidays -- and we were greatly excited when my Zaida came home one day and said, "Tomorrow we begin the woodwork." Of course, he, the kohen, was delighted with the rapid progress of the building, but he, the carpenter, had an even greater reason to rejoice for he was in charge of all the woodwork to be done in the new Shul (Synagogue).

My cousin Henny and I, who were playing in the kitchen, were excited. "May we go with you tomorrow, Zaida?" I asked. We held our breath.

"If you get up early, wash and say your morning prayers properly you may come along," he replied.

✡ ✡ ✡

It was a fine June morning and we hurried to keep up with our Zaida's long strides. No one could know our joy -- our Zaida was building the Shul and we were going to help him. Who was our equal?

All that day we played in the shteeber, the special pews or "houses" being readied for the elders of the congregation. We collected the sweet-smelling blond curls of planed wood and twisted them into our own blond and black hair.

We played house, amassing mounds of sawdust which served as sugar, salt and pepper in the "soup" we were cooking, each of us a mother in her own house. Our babies were dolls made from rolled-up towels, sleeping in their shoe-box carriages, drawn by a bit of string from last week's laundry. The sound of hammer, saw, plane and childhood prattle mingled with the echo from the skylight in the dome-shaped ceiling.

"See those ladders of light coming through the windows? They're for the angels and the prophet Elijah -- when they visit," Zaida pointed with a smile.

Our Zaida worked with a will. The smoke from his homemade cigarettes rose in spires like incense; the melodies he hummed reached out to us and drew us into the magic circle of his pleasure.

How well I remember the preparations for the first holiday celebration! It was Simchat Torah, the celebration of the Giving of the Ten Commandments to the Children of Israel at Mt. Sinai, the holiday which falls on the last night of Succot, the Feast of Tabernacles.

"On that night," Zaida informed us, "we read the last chapter of the Torah, followed immediately by the first chapter of Genesis to remind us that the Torah has no end."

All that week we had shared the excitement as Mamma and my Auntie Sheindle worked on the new mantles for the Holy Scrolls. They had shopped and compared silks and satins and were now decorating the shiny white mantles with gold braid Stars of David and bindings to match. We children had been busy preparing our flags for the synagogue procession, flags with the Lion of Judah emblazoned in blue and gold, flags attached to long sticks at the top of which we would put a polished red McIntosh apple with a small candle in it.

Dressed in white starched dresses which stood out stiffly over even more stiffly starched petticoats, Henny and I marched proudly to Shul with Zaida. Joyously we turned the corner onto St. Dominique Street, joining the throng of parents and children carrying, like us, small flags with polished apples and small coloured candles at the top. We would follow the elders as they circled the Synagogue with the Torahs in their arms so everyone could see the Holy Scrolls and kiss them with joy.

How beautiful the Synagogue appeared that night! I looked with awe at the twelve signs of the Zodiac painted onto the sky-blue wall above which rose the curtains cutting off the women's balcony. The new electric chandelier threw soft yellow lights on the freshly-varnished benches where we sat with Zaida. In the centre stood the Bimah, the raised platform, facing the east, Jerusalem, and the Ark of the Covenant with the Torah scrolls. The Rabbi, the Cantor and the choir greeted the incoming multitude from this place of honour. What exaltation! Could the Temple in Jerusalem have been lovelier?

In the women's balcony I thought for a moment I could see my Bubbie in her shining black Sabbath best with her fine black lace shawl over her freshly dressed peruke. I knew that through the curtain she was straining her eyes to see us and Zaida.

The fragrance of brandy being poured into thimble-sized goblets filled the air. "L'chaim! L'chaim!" the men cried to each other (To life!). I could hardly wait for the procession to begin.

Now it was time for the procession. "Line up, Gentlemen," called the Beadle, "it's time for Hakofess!"

The men chosen for the first honours pressed forward to the hand-polished Ark to receive their precious cargoes. The Beadle parted the Ark's gold-embroidered velvet curtains, the loving work of the women. As Zaida's hand-planed doors slid open, my heart grew tight within me. I grasped my flag more closely. There stood the Torahs in their new satin mantles which Mamma and Auntie had made. One even wore a silver crown with little golden bells and a silver breastplate!

Suddenly I heard my Zaida's name. "Harishon (First) Hakohen Baruch ben Tsion ...!" He, my Zaida, would lead the procession! He came forward, upright, smiling, his great prayer shawl upon his squared shoulders, his black skullcap framed in his silvering hair. Gently but firmly, he received into his arms -- not just *a* Torah, but *the* Torah, the Torah with the white satin mantle and the silver crown, the Torah with the magnificent silver breastplate and the little golden bells! The bells tinkled and my Zaida's eyes shone with pride, his lips turning up at the corners in pleasure.

The air grew heavy with the sweet smell of the brandy, the particular odour of the woolen prayer shawls, and the surge of humanity. The spirit of celebration and gratitude was everywhere in the Shul, in the Torah, in the congregation, in me.

The singing rose as the procession marched round the Bimah. "Ono Adonoi hoshiyo no! Ono Adonoi hatslicho no!" (Save us, Oh Lord, we beseech Thee! Prosper us, Oh Lord, we entreat Thee! Praised, praised be our Redeemer!)

We all pressed forward to touch and kiss the Torahs as they passed and to wish each celebrant, "Derlebt ibber ayor!" (May you live to carry the Torah again next year, next Simchas Torah!)

As he led the procession, the Shechinah, the Holy Spirit, seemed to rest upon my Zaida, the kohen, the carpenter. By the grace of the Almighty he had had a share in the building of this Mokom Kodesh, this holy place, and I knew as I looked at him that I was not only the granddaughter of a kohen, but of a Kohen Godol.

I Find My Jewish Name

One wintry Sunday night I found myself with my parents and other members of the family in the Monument National Theatre on St. Lawrence Boulevard, The Main. We were attending the graduation exercises of the Jewish Peretz Shule, the afternoon Yiddish school then known as the Natsionale Radicale Shule. The auditorium was packed with parents, friends and well-wishers, and an extravaganza had been mounted for the occasion -- a musical rendition of Joseph and his Brethren.

On stage, in the semi-darkness, the world of the Bible opened before me. There in the green fields of Canaan, amid sheaves of corn, Joseph the Dreamer appeared in his Coat of Many Colours and was denounced by his brothers for his arrogant dreams. The lights changed and in a torrid flood of colour, the unwitting Joseph was attacked by those jealous brothers who threw him into the pit to die, his glorious coat rent and defiled with animal blood to deceive his devastated loving father.

The boy pleaded for mercy, but the wicked brothers were adamant and poor Joseph was left alone, his anguished voice rising out of the pit as the malevolent men turned away. Only the fortuitous arrival of a caravan -- so the singing voice of Reuben told us -- saved the day, and he, Reuben, the eldest, pleaded with the others to sell the lad to the traders lest Joseph's blood be on their heads.

I was in another world as scene after scene filled the stage with colour, music, and heart-rending melodrama. Finally, the performance drew to a close as the Viceroy Joseph, in his purple cloak and golden coronet, enfolded his beloved father in his arms and offered forgiveness to his amazed repentant brothers -- and the curtain fell.

The audience went wild with applause. Exultant fathers and mothers ran to the stage with bouquets of flowers and boxes of candy for their so-gifted progeny, much to the anguish of those others who were not so rewarded for their efforts. The crowd milled around, everyone congratulating everyone else on the success of the evening. I clung to my Mamma's arm as something in me thundered, "This is mine! This is mine! I, too, must one day be a part of the wonderful world of the Shule."

In my Bubbie's house that memory was constantly reinforced by the Yiddish songs sung by my young aunts and uncles, songs they brought home from the Shule or from the Jewish Culture Clubs they attended. I pleaded with Mamma to let me go to Shule too, and great was my joy when she told me one September morning in my eighth year that I was to go to Shule now.

I could hardly wait for the afternoon at Strathearn School to come to an end. I ran home, rushed through my snack of milk and bread and jam and, heart high, floated all the way to Shule to attend my four o'clock class.

In the twilit room I took my place beside another little girl at a wooden double desk. Before us on the wall hung an enormous photograph of a large moustached gentleman with deep dark eyes and a wise friendly smile. He wore a black buttoned coat with narrow lapels and a stiff white collar. A tuft of dark hair fell over his high forehead towards his shaggy right eyebrow. I liked him at once.

"Who is this?" I nudged my small neighbour.

"That's Mr. Peretz. It's his school."

The teacher, a winsome young woman with smiling eyes, greeted us in Yiddish from her platform. "Some of you were not here when classes started the other day so I'll repeat what I told the class then," she said.

She told us that her name was Lerern Sherr. "Lerern means a lady teacher," she explained. Then she went on to say how glad she was to have so many new children in her class and promised that we would have a good time together and learn many things. She pointed to the picture of the nice man on the wall.

"This is the great Yiddish writer, Yitschak Labish Peretz for whom the school was named. He is no longer alive, but he wrote many wonderful poems and stories in his lifetime. You will learn some of them, just as he hoped you would." I felt she was speaking directly to me. "And perhaps, some day," she continued, "you, too, will write wonderful poems and stories for other children to enjoy."

I swallowed her every word, her every gesture. Here I belonged. If only the classes weren't held so late in the day!

"Now," said Lerern Sherr, "I will call the roll and you will answer 'Doh', which means Present. If you attended the singing class on Saturday afternoon you will say 'Geven', which means that you were there. And if you have done your homework, you will say, 'Gemacht'. Remember: 'Doh, geven, gemacht'."
"Dovid?"
"Doh, gemacht."
"Channah?"
"Doh, geven, gemacht."
"Baile?"
"Doh, geven, gemacht."
"Raizl?"
"Doh."
"Chaim?"
"Doh, gemacht."
"Sophie?"

There was a lull. It was me she was calling but I could not answer. Everyone had Jewish name but I! For what sort of Jewish name was Sophie or even Sophele? I burst into tears, my head on the wooden desk.

The teacher and the children were distressed. "What's the matter?" everyone asked. "Are you not feeling well?" Lerern Sherr wanted to know.

"No," I wailed. "I -- I don't have a Jewish name!"

The children looked at one another in dismay. Miss Sherr came down from her platform. Her gentle voice encompassed me. "Don't cry," she comforted me, an arm around my shoulder. "I'm sure you have a Jewish name. Ask your mother."

At home I looked accusing into Mamma's eyes. "Everyone in Shule has a Jewish name except me!" I attacked. "Sophela! Sophela!" I scoffed at myself bitterly.

"But of course you have a Jewish name!" Mamma replied. "Your name is Shulamis, for my father Shloime."

"Then why do you call me Sophela?"

"We live in Canada. We wanted you to have an English name for school. Sophia was a famous woman, a Russian Socialist ...."

But who cared for Russia, for Socialism, for Fame?

"Shulamis! Shulamis!" The air was filled with music as I repeated it again and again. I was no longer an outcast in my own heart. I belonged and I had a Jewish name like all the other children in the class -- and such a lovely singing name!

In Shule next day, as I brought the glad tidings to the class, I was several cubits taller.

"Shulamis?" said the teacher. "What a lovely name! Shulamis is the sweetheart of King Solomon in the Shir Hashirim, the Song of Songs."

There was mixed reaction to her reply. Some of the children remained wide-eyed, open-mouthed with wonder, others sniggered ....

And I? I was transported with joy and unfathomable memory! And while in the Protestant school I continued to be known as Sophie, I was Shulamis, she of the singing name, the little girl who lived on Colonial Avenue near Prince Arthur -- and the Sweetheart of King Solomon.

A new dimension was added to my life. Within the walls of the Shule, I learned that the Sabbath was for singing, and that before my ancestors lived in Russia I had ancestors who had lived in Spain, in Babylon, in Egypt and in the golden Promised Land. There too, I learned of a return to Zion, of lasting friendships, of responsibility to the community in which I lived, and of love. From the thread that started spinning on that magical night in the Monument National Theatre, I began to weave a Coat of Many Colours of my own.

Yiddish writer Y.L. Peretz, 1852-1915, for whom the Peretz Shule was named. His works have been translated into English and other languages.

Papa Finds a Country

Every spring Papa made his pilgrimage to the Laurentians "to find a country". Soon after Passover, when the snow had begun to disappear and the days to lengthen, Mamma would begin her incantation: "Soon will be summer. Where will we go? We have to look for a Kontra. We have to find a place for the summer ...."

On the first promising Sunday, Papa would take the 9 a.m. train at Mile End Station and go as far as Ste. Agathe. He would hunt in and around the neighbouring villages of the Jewish summer ghetto, seeking out farmers who rented out cottages or moved into their summer kitchens for the season and rented out their own houses for whatever they would bring.

Since there was no transportation in these little villages, it was important to rent from a farmer who could undertake to supply his tenants with fresh milk, eggs and vegetables from his own farm. There was also the anticipation of the buggy ride Mamma would arrange for us with the farmer once a year, a treat which always made the summer memorable.

That Sunday morning, Mamma sent Papa off with the usual catalogue of specific instructions: "Remember, Philip -- a new house. With a good stove. And the pump should work easy. And it should be near the train and near the river for swimming. And not too deep for the children. And not too far from the village; they should be able to go for mail every day. And with a good farmer with a horse and buggy -- he should deliver and take us sometimes for a drive ...."

My little sister Denie and I stood by full of excitement. She was a loving little girl and I had grown very protective of her. As the day ahead seemed endless to us, I said, "Denie, let's go play outside."

We joined the children on the street. My friends Bessie and Sarah were trying to play skip rope with another girl. The boys kept interfering, jumping in to "catch a free skip". Bessie was threatening them with the rope. "Get away from here, ya hear? I'll smack ya with the handles!" We ran to join in the fun.

Denie couldn't contain herself. "Our father's gone to look for a country!" she announced.

"So?" said Bessie, raising her chin defiantly. "He finds you a country and you miss all the fun in the city!"

But Denie didn't hear. "It's so good there ..," she rambled on, "it's green all over and smells so good with Christmas trees!"

"Yeh, sure!" scoffed Bessie enviously again.

"You have fun here and we have fun there," I countered. "You remember last year I sent you a letter on birch bark from the trees there? And we made a concert with the other children and we danced Roses, Roses and sang The Make Belief Forever just like in school by the gym concert ...."

"All right! All right! Ya wanna skip or no?" Bessie cut us off. "You and Sarah take an end. I'll skip first." And as we turned rope, she began to intone, acting out the rhyme as she skipped,

Teddy Bear Teddy Bear
turn around
Teddy bear Teddy Bear
touch the ground
Teddy Bear Teddy Bear
show your shoe
Teddy Bear Teddy Bear
one-two-three *skidoo!*

"Now pepper!" she shouted.

I quickened the rope. "Faster! Faster!" she shouted. The rope smacked the hot sidewalk with the speed of an eggbeater. Suddenly Sarah called, "Bessie, you're out! You're next, Sophie."

Even as I skipped, I was out there somewhere with Papa on the train, on the country roads viewing the empty summer cottages which were waiting for us and for other children to bring them to life.

"Sophie Borodensky, what's the matter with you!" Bessie's bark suddenly cut the air. "It's *pepper* already! You're out!"

Toward evening, Papa returned exhausted but content.

"I found a kontra," he reported. "A beauty. New. In Belisle's Mills. Near the river. Not far from the train. A sandy beach. Good for swimming and a few houses for neighbors. And not far from a hotel."

We all smiled happily at him.

"How many rooms?" asked Mamma.

"How many rooms?" Papa hesitated. "Seven," he finally said.

Mamma's eyes bulged. "Seven rooms!? Madness! Madness -- on my enemies' heads! I need seven rooms? I'll kill myself!"

"It's a beautiful house. The best I saw," Papa pleaded.

Mamma was livid. "So? I need seven rooms? What will I do with them? Who'll clean them?"

"You'll rent out two rooms, like by other people."

"I need tenners? Women around the stove?" Mamma clasped her hands in consternation. "Such a big house! Who'll look after it?"

"This is the last time I go look for a kontra!" Papa exploded in one of the few times I heard him raise his voice. He threw himself into a heap on the large red leather armchair. "I do my best to please you. I come back tired like a dog and you're not satisfied! You'll hire a girl and you'll take the children and you'll go to the kontra -- or else stay home! I'm finished, you hear? Finished!"

Mamma sulked for a day, then spoke on the phone for the next couple of days and rented out two rooms to two ladies with good recommendations from other ladies with whom they had previously shared houses. "If they can get along with them, so can I," she announced. "I can get along with anyone!" And she gave Papa a meaningful look.

We waited eagerly for the school year to come to an end. The day school let out, a truck picked up our trunks, and next morning at nine, Mamma, Denie, the newly hired maid Winnie, and I boarded the train for Val David, Quebec, then known as Belisle's Mills.

This was the first of many wonderful summers in Belisle's Mills. Oh, those summers with the Laurentian Mountains gently ringing the Valley like a porridge bowl, rainbows and sunsets throwing stained-glass reflections on their green craggy sides, fragrant fields of hay and clover, wildflowers unnamed until I had named them. There was always that first taste of wild strawberries (Zemlieniki Mamma called them) and the raspberries, blueberries and blackberries which appeared in succession for our pleasure during the eight weeks we spent there, and the fragrance of the boiling fruit turning to jam or jelly on the woodstove, liquid sunshine which filled the many quarts of tightly sealed mason jars which Papa took home every Sunday night to fill the pantry shelves for our winter's delight. Zaida always spent part of the summer with us, as did our young aunts who came for their vacation.

We grew and flourished. I improved my swimming. Denie learned to swim. We rose early and went to bed with the birds. The farmer kept his promise and delivered fresh vegetables, milk and often still-warm eggs. Mamma rested in the afternoon sun and enjoyed the companionship of the other women while we played with the children in the yard. On Tuesday mornings Mamma would say, "Today we write letters to Papa," and she wrote the same letter every week:

Dear Philip, we are well and hope to hear the same from you. Everything here is the same. Please bring with you when you come ....

Then followed the list of the many things he should bring. I, in her image, added our letter:

Dear Papa, We are well. We're having a good time. How are you? Please bring us ....

On Saturday night Papa would arrive with two heavy valises full of fruit and other seasonable delectables, supplies which we could not get in the country store or from the farmer. There was always the box of Laura Secord Chocolates, one piece to be enjoyed after lunch every day instead of the two cents for candy we received at home during the school year. Papa would join us at berry picking, at swimming and at all our meals. How good it was to be together.

"I wish summer could be forever," Denie often whispered at the end of such days. "Me too," I nodded, already looking to the next weekend.

As I look back, all those summers fade into one nostalgic sameness, a sameness broken only by the awareness of the lengthening of our shoes, of the budding of our breasts, and of the slow awakening of girlhood hungers, or by their aftermath -- like the aftermath of that first summer which had brought us Winnie through whom we learned that there was loud joyous laughter -- and also that there was sorrow in the world.

Winnie

Winnie was the first of a long line of maids who stayed with us in my childhood home. Finding the right maid wasn't easy, but Mamma was always ailing and someone had to do the housework, shop for things that were not delivered to the house and, in general, do Mamma's bidding. Winnie shared our room. She slept in the single bed by the window and Denie and I shared a three-quarter bed.

She came to us at the end of May, about a month before we went to the country that summer. I didn't take to Winnie. She was a big strapping country girl from New Brunswick who spoke only French, laughed loudly and heartily, and offered up prayers to a strange God who favoured beads and crosses -- a totally different God from my grandmother's. Winnie came on the heels of a girl who had been dismissed after her first afternoon in our house. She had locked herself in the bathroom for a long time and Mamma was worried.

"Find out what she's doing there so long," urged my auntie who had dropped in for an afternoon cup of tea. "You don't know who she is. After all, you have young children in the house ...."

When the girl came out of the bathroom carrying a rubber bag with a long tube and a box of medication in her hands, Mamma was doubly distressed. She phoned the druggist, Mr. Schmerling, who sent his message boy for the medication, and I later heard Mamma tell Papa over the phone, "He says it's a medicine for women who have to do with men."

"In that case," said Papa (as I again heard Mamma tell my auntie), "pay her for the day and let her go right away."

The next day Mamma hired Winnie.

Winnie came with clear demands: she would be paid twenty dollars a month, have Thursday afternoons and second Sundays off and be free to go home for Christmas with pay.

When I told my friend Bessie that we had a French maid, she bristled. "Why a French? They hate the Jews worst then the English. They're Cath'lics -- like the nuns. Why doesn't your mother get a English -- you should be able to talk to her?"

"They don't answer the advertisement. Only the French. That's why. And my father says there's good and bad people by everyone. And anyways, I could learn French."

Winnie's large white teeth and hearty laugh frightened me, but Mamma took to her, except that she was horrified by Winnie's appetite. "I just bought a half-peck apples yesterday by Mr. Umansky," she told Papa the next day, "and they're all gone already. And a kimmel bread with butter and jam she ate up this afternoon with tea."

"Leave her," said Papa, remembering his hungry days as an apprentice to a tailor in the Old Country. "She'll eat till she's full, then she'll stop. You'll see."

Hard as it was for Mamma, she controlled herself and Winnie stayed on because she worked well and made Mamma laugh without language, but with funny gestures. She quickly picked up some words from Mamma's defective English and before long we felt that Winnie was here to stay.

✡ ✡ ✡

In Belisle's Mills Winnie was in her element. She loved the country. She never seemed to be lonely. She was cheerful, sang her French-Canadian songs, and loved to whistle. She was a magician with the woodstove despite the early-morning damp wood, and was a whiz at priming the pump and getting the wicks in the coal-oil lamps to burn without smoking. Our wooden floors shone under her mop and the other women appreciated her help. She soon made friends with the French-Canadian help at the nearby Jewish hotel and at the end of every day, she made her way through the woods to laugh with the young folk who spoke her own language.

Denie and I had little to do with her. She was our mother's maid and that was that. She slept in the large unfinished attic, and we were never allowed to intrude into her domain. We were just as happy not to, for we had heard the flapping of wings there and were scared as Winnie, who didn't know the English name for the creatures, laughed her loud toothsome laugh, ogled us with wide protruding eyes, flapped her hands, thumbs close to her temples and made a strange muffled sound.

"Bats," Mamma said. "Madame Dufresne says bats fly around here and sometimes they hide in the attic in dark corners."

"She'll have to cut off all her hair!" I cried, covering my own with my hands in horror as I remembered the rhyme I had picked up from the other children: Bats in the hair -- no longer fair ....

Winnie laughed. "Me no 'fraid," she spoke her newly acquired phrases. "Me ketch'm coup coup!" she continued, motioning two sharp blows with the edge of her palm on the creatures' imaginary necks. "Puis -- bam-bam -- sur la porte. Bonne chance. For luck!" she roared again. I shuddered as I recalled the spread-winged mouselike creatures on Farmer Dufresne's barn door.

I envied Winnie. I envied her her lusty laughter, her ability to make Mamma laugh, her grown-up fun with the farmer's son, Jehosephat, her general ease in the world. Mamma's constant ailing had turned me inward and I envied Winnie so much that one day I stole seven cents from her purse. I was too frightened to spend it and threw it into the river, but Winnie was aware of the robbery and let me know she knew. While she said nothing to Mamma, there existed a terrible bond between us.

On Thursday afternoons, Mamma played bridge at the Jewish hotel. The games were arranged to raise funds for Jewish charities. There was a shortcut through the forest from our house to the hotel. It was a lovely trodden path, bordered by wild ferns, tall pines and birches, with soft green turf and red berries cushioning the ground on both sides. To others it was only a shortcut, but to me it was a magical road.

Each time I walked along that path I mesmerized myself by peering up high into the treetops to see where the sun hung or by searching out the stars and the changing moon. Whenever my eyes returned to the path again, I was sure I would meet a wonderful stranger -- like in the fairy tales I was reading -- not necessarily on a white horse on such a narrow path, but a fine stranger -- a Prince -- who would tell me of his wanderings and would be able to solve all riddles. We couldn't be married right away, nor could he take me at once to his far-off castle, but he would leave me with a promise that in a few years, when he had solved his three riddles, etc. etc.... It was a lovely place.

One Thursday afternoon, Mamma had gone to attend the weekly fund-raising bridge party at the hotel. It was also Winnie's afternoon off. I had stayed around the house playing with the other children. As dusk began to fall, I had suddenly grown wistful and decided to go find Mamma.

As I entered the woods, I thought I heard a low moaning. I stopped and listened. It wasn't a bird. It wasn't the wind. I could see nothing. The moaning stopped for a short while and I continued into the woods.

Suddenly it started again in waves of growing intensity and I was frightened. I looked back to find I was more than halfway through the woods. I couldn't turn back. As I took a step forward, I let out a wild shriek. There, behind a copse in the twilight, was a ghost -- a real ghost -- waving its arms heavy with flowing whiteness and moaning; moaning in terrifying anguish, "OOOOOOOOO! Oooooooo! OOOOOOOO!"

I froze in my steps. "Mamma! Mamma!" I shrieked in unfamiliar tones. "Mamma! Mamma!"

The ghost seemed to take a step toward me. "Monee ... Moneeeee," the ghost wailed at me!

"No! No more!" I shrieked again. "Mamma! Mamma!"

A roar of laughter filled the air. It was Winnie robed in a sheet. "Jus' pour le fun!" she roared. "Don' yell! C'est jus' pour le fun." And she came forward, pulling off the sheet and laughing wildly.

She took me home and fed me cold milk and bread with jam.

✡ ✡ ✡

When Mamma came home I was in bed. My eyes were red with crying.

"What happened?" Mamma asked. Winnie stood behind her, smiling in the doorway.

"It was dark in the shortcut and I got frightened ... but Winnie came and took me home."

"There's nothing to be afraid of in these woods, is there Winnie?" Mamma asked, looking first at me and then at the smiling maid.

"No. Never. Just ghosts!" And she roared again.

Silently I shook my head. We were even and I was free.

Denie Prepares for School

That summer Denie just couldn't wait for the season to end.

"When will it be Labour Day already?" she kept asking. Neither the fresh young corn from our farmer's garden, nor the heavy crop of wild blackberries that flourished that summer could compensate. Even Mamma's repeated praise as she quickly converted our take into jars and jars of purple-red translucent jelly didn't satisfy. As the August rains came down and the houses emptied of their summer guests, Denie asked the same question every day: "When will be Labour Day? It's getting so empty in the yard ...."

"It's better in the country," Mamma said. "The air is fresh -- and we paid till Labour Day."

Papa brought a calendar and Mamma invited Denie to cross off each day as bedtime came around.

"See? Not so long already," Mamma finally announced. "Sunday Papa will help us pack and Monday is Labour Day and we go home."

"And Tuesday," Denie rejoined, "we go write me into school!"

"May it be in a lucky hour!" Mamma blessed devoutly.

"I'll take you," I volunteered. "I'll take you to the office and *unroll* you," I corrected her Yiddishism.

During that last week ours was the only inhabited house in the area. Fortunately the weather had turned hot and clear and we spent most of our time swimming or visiting the empty cottages in search of possible treasures the occupants might have left behind. Thus the week ran by more quickly than we had expected and on Labour Day, our arms laden with Golden Glow flowers, a gift from our farmer who had come to say good-bye, we boarded the noon train for the pleasant journey home.

✡ ✡ ✡

The first leaves on the maple across from our house on Colonial Avenue were already turning red. As we got out of the taxi, the hot smell of the dusty street hit us. We looked about for our friends. The street was deserted. On some of the stoops before open doors, gray-faced neighbours sat scantily clad, waiting for the evening to bring a reprieving wind.

Suddenly, a familiar raucous voice cut the air.

"Sarah, hey! Look who's here!" Bessie was waving to us from her stairs. "It's Sophie and Denie back from the country!" We waved back happily.

"Boy! Ya missed some summer!" she called as they came running towards us.

"You look so sunburnt!" Sarah admired. "You had fun in the country?"

"Yeh." We were delighted to see our friends. "We had fun. You?"

Denie bubbled over. "We went swimming and picked berries. It was nice there."

"Too bad your mother is always sick and you always have to go to the country. Ya missed *some* fun here," Bessie tantalized us to assuage her envy. "We went on Fletcher's Field every Sunday. We took a picnic: hard eggs and chicken and bread and jam. And my mother took the samovar for tea. We had fun ...."

"And the other days?" I asked, not knowing how much to envy her.

"It wasn't so much fun," Sarah contradicted her. "It was hot and sticky and even if we went to Shubert's Bath on Main Street, it was still hot! I'm glad you were in the country," she added lovingly.

"Maybe next year you could come too ...," I offered putting my arm around my friend's shoulder. "Next year we could have fun together."

"We came home to write me in in school tomorrow," Denie's smile lit all her freckles to a glow. "I have to go in Kindergarten."

"Ya mean we have to *unroll* you," Bessie corrected as I had done. "Good. So we'll all go with you to the office in the morning."

"Bessie! You know the office teacher won't let ...," Sarah intervened. "You know only those that *need* can go to the office. It gets too crowdy."

"So all right. We'll walk together to school in the morning," Bessie compromised. "But you should be early, ya hear? I want to be first in line. Eight o'clock. Ya hear?"

Denie lit up again. The whole world revolved about her.

In the morning Denie prodded me.

"Sophie, you're asleep?"

"Yeh. What time is it?" I heard her as through a dream.

"I look nice?" she asked.

"What time is it?" My eyes were still shut. "The alarm went off already?"

"It didn't have to. I was awake."

I opened one eye and glanced at the clock. "Denie, it's not even seven o'clock yet! Why are you dressed so early? Come to bed!"

"I can't! I have on my new school dress and my patten leather shoes. I couldn't sleep so I got dressed. It's in the morning already. We have to go to school early to *unroll* me. Remember?" Denie emphasized the word to show she remembered.

"It's so early! I want to sleep yet." I retreated under the cover.

"Sophie," she prodded me lightly again. "You remember today you have to write me in?" The repressed excitement in her voice touched me. I rubbed my eyes and sat up in bed.

"You look so nice, Denie," I smiled through the morning blur. "The teacher will like you ...."

As I brushed my teeth I heard Papa fixing the cocoa for our breakfast. Mamma in her green and yellow bathrobe, joined me in the bathroom.

"It's a nice sunny day," she said softly. "I can't believe it. Already both my children in school. The house will be empty."

Through the open windows we heard the excitement on the street. "Not yet eight o'clock," Mamma noted. "What's their hurry? They should only want to go to school like this later in the year ...."

Denie was too excited to eat. "I can't. My belly feels funny!" she pleaded.

"You have to eat. A person has to have strength for school. You see the surprise Papa made for you? Cocoa and French toast. Eat. Eat. A new beginning is a special occasion. You have to treat it with respect."

"Mamma, let her just drink the cocoa," I tried to hurry them along from the doorway. "She could take the French toast for recess." Denie gave me a mournful look as she gulped down the hot drink.

Mamma couldn't seem to let Denie go. Every time she said goodbye and reached for the door, Mamma called her back.

"Dinyela, I'll fix the bow in back of your dress."

"Dinyela, you forgot your hanky. Come. I'll pin it on for you."

"Dinyela, your hair ribbon isn't straight. A suchy year on me, on us all -- like the sun shines on your golden head ...."

I grew impatient. "Mamma, it's past eight already! They won't wait for us."

There was a struggle for control in Mamma's voice. "It's only eight o'clock!" she managed, adding sadly, "the time flies ... both children in school already ...." She walked to the door calling after us, "Go in good health! You should both have a good year, dear God. It should be a good beginning! We should all be well and Papa and I should only have pleasure from you ...."

I Unroll Denie in School

I

"Bessie, wait for me! I'm coming!" I shouted from our balcony to my friend who was already walking away.

"You're slow like molasses! I'm not waiting!" Bessie was her own lovable self. "You're some sister! Ya havta unroll your own little sister in school today, and you're not even ready!"

"It's not me! It's my mother! She's saying good-bye to Denie still! We're coming, we're coming!"

Denie and I rushed down the stairs and caught up with the stream of children heading toward Prince Arthur Street en route to Strathearn School.

"Ya know I want to be first in line!" Bessie continued to scold. And to Denie, "So Mazal Tov, Denie. First time in school, eh? I hope ya get a good teacher, not a crank. My first teacher was just terrible. She made us sit stiff in class and ya couldn't go to the toilet. Only by recess. Yer glad yer going?"

But Denie was too excited to speak or care. She skipped along happily, singing, "I'm going to school, my new shoes squeak."

Bessie overheard. "New shoes for school, eh? By us we get new shoes for Yontif," she referred to the High Holidays and Passover. "It's more important than for school."

We were all first generation Canadians. Yiddish was the language of our homes with Russian or Polish used by our elders to convey information not for children's ears. Our first break with our parental ties were the English names given us by older siblings or teachers upon registration in the Protestant school. It was the baptism of Anglicization where the names of saints, of Greek gods and goddesses, and of Anglo-Saxon heroes replaced the Jewish names given at birth to commemorate deceased parents or other relatives or friends. Thus Chaya (life) became Catherine -- a good Catholic name, Chaim became Hyman (a Greek god), Ita-Bayla became Isabelle, Yitschak became Issie, Isadore, or Irving, and my Uncle Laibl became Lloyd. Thus my own name, Shulamis, honouring my maternal grandfather, Shloime, had become Sophie.

The thought of changing Denie's name had never occurred to me. She had been named Dena Rochel for a great-aunt, and everyone called her Denie.

"Waddaya gonna call her in school?" Bessie wanted to know.

"Denie. Her name is Denie. That's her name."

"They won't let. You'll see. You'll have to change it."

Bessie's brother Hymie interrupted our discussion. "Hey, Willie!" he shouted to a boy across the street. "Ya gonna be in my class?"

"Maybe," Willie shouted back. "Issie can't. He's not pimoded."

"Yeh, the teacher didn't like me!" Issie defended himself.

"Some teacher ya had!" Hymie abetted. "A real ...."

"Don't say it!" Bessie interrupted from our side of the street. "If I tell Ma you called the teacher a dirty name, you'll get it."

Everyone walked along happily, dressed in his best for the occasion. Deeply implanted were the respect for learning, the magical hope for "a good beginning", and the desire to make a good impression on the new teacher and on friends.

"So waddlya call her?" Bessie asked again.

Denie, completely euphoric, clung tightly to my hand as we marched along. In her off-tune little voice she sang the song she had made up on the spur of the moment,

> Today is school, first day school.
> My new shoes squeak, my new shoes squeak ....

"Come faster," Bessie goaded again. "I told ya I wanna be first in line today!"

II

Strathearn School was located on Jeanne Mance above Prince Arthur in the English neighbourhood on the west side of St. Lawrence Main. Prince Arthur was the street of little Jewish groceries and service stores, but Jeanne Mance wore an aura of elegance. Tall trees lined its sidewalks, and fine two-storey limestone dwellings with bay windows, little gardens, and long flights of outdoor wooden stairs with wrought iron banisters marked it for good living. Up one flight, a little beyond the school, lived my last year's teacher, next door to where the Grade Three teacher who died from scarlet fever had lived. Around the block -- this we only dared whisper to each other -- lived the principal, and two streets east lived the "Office Teacher" -- the educational supervisor.

Strathearn School was new and beautiful. It was a four-storey brick building. Its bright classrooms with their large windows and freshly varnished desks invited learning. To most of us children it was the most splendid building we had ever seen.

Ninety-eight percent of the school population was Jewish and there were two Jewish teachers on the staff of thirty-five. Classes were co-educational, but boys and girls congregated in separate basements with separate toilet facilities.

Denie was impressed -- no, thrilled. So thrilled that she immediately had to go to the toilet. Unaware of the facilities, she fretted.

"We have to go home. I have to make ...."

"No." I smiled at her naiveté. "We go here."

She was delighted with the small toilets hidden in individual cubicles behind short wooden doors -- the roll of white toilet paper unknown to her as it had been to all of us until we entered school, with the small sinks in which to wash our hands and with the roller towels to dry them. In a word, everything was new, everything delighted her. Even the feet beneath the stalls intrigued her.

"Look," she said, "shoes. All kinds shoes. Even big brown oxfords like yours ...." We smiled happily at each other and hand in hand returned to the basement to join my last year's line and await the bells.

Our principal was a fine gentleman of handsome bearing. He was soft-spoken, grandfatherly, and ran the school with discipline and decorum. Everyone feared, loved and respected him. He took special delight in teaching us good manners and neatness. Just before bell time, he appeared in the basement and moved quietly among the thronging children, slowing them down, pointing with his cane to a piece of paper or a bit of orange peel on the floor and to the large metal garbage bin. A nod from him was a command. Thanks to the standards he set, and to our ever-sweeping caretaker, our basement and school were always tidy despite the hundreds of children who milled there all day.

With the first bell there appeared at the head of the stairs a drummer boy in Boy Scout attire, drum and sticks at attention.

With the second bell, the children moved into their respective classroom groups, in columns, two by two, led by the Grade Seven girls who were supposed to set an example. The third bell signaled the drummer to beat an advance and proudly and rhythmically, we marched silently upstairs to our various rooms to the spirited rat-a-tat of the drum. The mood was broken only by the authoritative voice of monitors who called out at intervals, "Stop whispering in line or I take you to the office!"

Happily dragging my bedazzled Denie by the hand, I reached the door of my classroom.

"Please, Miss," I addressed my teacher, "this is my little sister Denie. I have to write her in today."

"You have to what?" she asked in genteel tones.

"I have to write her in. I mean *unroll* her. She needs to go to Kindergarten."

"You mean you want to register her. You may take her to the office."

At the office, a long line of children was waiting to be registered. They waited with parents or with older siblings. We joined them. "Let's wait here by the lockers," I directed. "You have to stand on the white line with your toes together."

We waited.

The office teacher, Miss Bradshaw, sat at her desk "writing in" the new children. The lady before us had brought a little boy from Scotland. His name was Donald MacGlashen. Miss Bradshaw smiled, greeted the mother graciously and commented, "From the Auld Country. How nice! Donald will do well here. We're glad to have him." She proceeded with the registration.

"And who is this?" she asked me as Mrs. MacGlashen left.

"It's my sister Denie." I pushed Denie forward with pride.

"What's your name, little girl?" she addressed Denie.

"I'm Denie."

"Jeanie?"

"No. Denie. Denie Borodensky. My father and mother come from the Old Country too," Denie offered her credentials. Miss Bradshaw smiled. Suddenly she seemed to have something in her left eye -- an unseen speck which she tried to wipe out as her right hand covered her face. "Really? How nice. What is your name in

English?" Denie turned to me. I froze. What other name could Denie have?

"Her English name," Miss Bradshaw repeated, turning to me.

Suddenly I was inspired. At the Globe Theatre on Saturday afternoon we had cried ourselves sick over the movie The Orphans of the Storm. Oh, those poor little sisters, those brave little outcasts -- Lillian and Dorothy Gish! How beautifully they had suffered! Lillian and *Dorothy* Gish. Heaven is my witness -- her name began with a D!

"Her name is Dorothy," I announced proudly. "Dorothy, like by Lillian and Dorothy Gish ...."

"Dorothy?" Miss Bradshaw smiled. "And are you from the Old Country too?"

"No. I'm Denie from Colonial Avenue," she answered bravely.

"And you want to go to kindergarten?" Miss Bradshaw really liked Denie.

Denie beamed. "Yes."

"Then come with me, Dorothy," said Miss Bradshaw, gently taking Denie by the hand. "We'll go together. You may return to your classroom," she nodded to me.

And without so much as a wave of farewell, Denie, now Dorothy, disappeared down the long darkening corridor into the new world of Canadian English culture.

I Learn the Facts of Life

Another year had come and gone; another summer had passed. The new school term and the oncoming High Holidays absorbed our attention. Mamma and Winnie had stripped the summer throws off the furniture. Winnie had rolled the rugs onto the floors again. The freshly washed curtains lit up the rooms and the ice box and pantry were newly scrubbed and filled with the bounty of the harvest to greet the New Year. We children were delighted to find our friends again. With school and the after-school Jewish classes, we spent few waking hours at home.

Winnie was now part of our family. She worked, served and moved in and about our lives. But something about her had changed. She was no longer the loud, laughing, prank-playing country bumpkin we had known. Even Denie noticed it.

"Something is different with Winnie," I said to Denie one day.

"Yeh. She doesn't laugh like in the country .... What's the matter with her?"

"Maybe she's sick. Let's try to make her laugh."

"Winnie, make like a bat," I urged at supper, putting my hands to my temples and wagging my fingers as she had done. Winnie only turned and walked out of the room and I heard the lock turn in the bathroom. I was asleep when she came into the bedroom, and even in my sleep I thought I could hear Winnie weep.

Mamma too was perturbed.

"I don't know what's happened to her," I heard her say to Papa one day. "She's not the same at all since we're home."

"Maybe she misses her friends in the country. Maybe she's in love," Papa replied.

"Maybe I should talk to her ...." Mamma said. But when Mamma asked Winnie if anything was wrong, Winnie said no, and went about her work.

Auntie was the one to see the obvious. "Vichna," she said one day to Mamma, "your girl is pregnant."

"You're mad!" Mamma exploded. "You and your ideas!"

"I'm telling you she's pregnant," Auntie insisted. "Look at her breasts."

"You and your ideas!" Mamma repeated a little less convincingly.

But to Papa I heard her say, "I'm afraid your sister-in-law is right. Look at her breasts ...."

"And if she is, what can we do about it?" asked Papa.

What sort of talk is this? I wondered. "Papa, Winnie isn't even married!" I said. "How can she be pregnant?"

"Right," said Papa, patting my back as I stood before him. "Just don't you give it another thought. Have you finished your homework?"

I nodded.

"Then go to bed like a good girl. Good-night, dear."

As the weeks went on, I watched Winnie with ever-growing wonder and concern. Several times, when I came in unannounced, conversation between her and Mamma came to a sudden halt. Often during the night I heard Winnie weeping, but I didn't dare move lest I disturb her even more. She wasn't eating as much at mealtimes, yet she was certainly getting fatter.

Chanukah and Christmas were approaching. There would be holidays from school and festivities at home. Winnie, who on her arrival had stipulated that she must have the right to go home for Christmas, now made no mention of claiming that right.

"I want to see how you celebrate the holidays," she said when I asked her.

We lit the Chanukah candles those eight nights and received little bags with Chanukah money from Papa. Winnie got her little bag too, but she just stood sadly, nodded her head and said nothing. As Christmas drew nearer she began to make Christmas stockings for Denie and me. Mamma was distressed.

"Christmas stockings in a Jewish house? Crazy!" she remonstrated to Papa.

"Let her. She's unhappy. The children know it's not their holiday." There was no laughter in Winnie.

✡ ✡ ✡

"How much longer do you intend to keep her?" I heard my auntie ask Mamma one snowy afternoon as they were sipping the tea which Winnie had served them in the dining room. I was in the kitchen getting my milk and bread and jam before going to my Jewish classes.

"I don't know. She has nowhere to go. She doesn't want her family to know. I don't know what to do."

"Has she seen a doctor?"

"I took her to the clinic at the hospital last week. They say she's fine."

"What about the father?"

"They asked her. She refuses to say anything about him. I asked her too."

"So what will she do with the baby? She can't keep it!"

"The Social Service said she should give it to the nuns."

"So what did she say?"

"She began to cry. I must tell you -- I cried too," said Mamma.

The glass fell from my hand with a clatter. Then it was true! Winnie wasn't married and she was going to have a baby! And they were telling her to give the baby away!

"What's happening there?" Mamma called to me. "Better be more careful."

I didn't know whether to weep or to rejoice for Winnie. She was having a baby! How wonderful! But she would have to give it away! And how could a baby have no father? It was clear I wasn't to ask about that at home.

As usual, Bessie was my source of information. As we filed out at noon to get our coats from the lockers I called to her, "Bessie, walk home with me lunch time. I have to tell you something."

We shuffled through the snow banks on Prince Arthur Street but I couldn't bring myself to talk about Winnie. Bessie was soon impatient.

"So? Tell me already. What's the secret?"

"Bessie -- our maid Winnie -- she's got a baby ...."

"Yeh? So Mazl Tov! When did she get it? Boy or girl?"

"We don't know yet. It's still inside."

"Yeh? So where's her husband? He lives by you too?"

"No. She doesn't have any husband. She just got a baby."

Bessie stopped suddenly, one leg suspended. "Ya mean she fucked a boy and got pregning? Oy vay! When?"

"Naw, Bessie! Not like that! She's just very fat -- and I heard my mother tell my auntie the hospital wants -- "

"What d'ya mean, 'Not like that'? It's the only way! Ya dunno how ya get a baby? Ya fuck so ya get!"

"No, Bessie! Not our Winnie!" Everything in me was crying, *Not like that! That's dirty!* But to Bessie I said, "Stop it, Bessie. It's Winnie's baby. It's her own baby!"

"She must of got it in the country. Them farmer Frenchies -- they get lots of babies -- always. Boys. Girls. Whole gangs. Hmmmm."

"Bessie, I -- I wish we could keep that baby in our house."

"Ya crazy!" she blared. "A mumzer (bastard)! Jews don't like mumzers. My mother would throw her down the stairs!"

I ached for Winnie and her baby and spent restless nights worrying about them. Spring had begun to show itself and Winnie was very, very big. I heard Mamma say to Papa, "I'll have to get a woman in to wash the walls down for Passover." But Winnie wouldn't hear of it. One Tuesday afternoon, when Mamma went out, Winnie got the ladder and washed the dining-room walls. Mamma was horrified when she came in and caught her finishing the job.

"Winnie! It's not for you! I'll get someone else to do it!"

"I do my job, Madame," she said and burst out crying. "You so good for me!"

✡ ✡ ✡

One April night, just before Passover, Winnie woke suddenly with a moan.

"Winnie, what's wrong?" I asked.

"Dat all right. You sleep," she said softly, beginning to get dressed. She pulled a small valise from under her bed and went out of the room. I heard her muffled voice on the phone and then heard the door shut.

Next morning, Mamma greeted me at breakfast.

"Winnie had a baby. A boy. They just phoned from the hospital."

I trembled. "Mamma, can we see it -- the baby?"

"No. You go to school. I'll go visit her this afternoon and tell you about it after school."

Mamma visited Winnie every day at the Hopital Francais, now Jeanne d'Arc. She never went empty-handed. One evening she said to us, "I have good news. Winnie's baby is going home today -- to a very good home. No, not to Winnie's home, but to a nice family that has no children of their own."

"And Winnie?" I asked, my eyes full of tears.

"Winnie is going back to her parents' home for a while. One day she will marry and have other babies of her own."

"But why can't she stay by us?" I pleaded.

"I asked her, but she said she wants to go home."

We all went to see Winnie off. As we stood at the CPR station Denie and I were crying. Mamma was biting her lip. Papa gave Winnie a big box of chocolates "for the road" and carried her luggage onto the train. He seated Winnie at a window.

Winnie was weeping as she waved to us from the open window. "I never forget you!" she cried. "Never! Never!"

"Come back to us, Winnie," I called. "I'll never forget you too...!"

Denie Learns Sewing

A gray November afternoon. Bessie, Sarah and I waited for Denie in the basement of Strathearn School.

"How come we have to wait for her?" Bessie was impatient. "She knows it's Friday and I have to go home early to help my Mother make Shabbess (prepare for the Sabbath). And now it gets dark early."

"Maybe her teacher picked her to help," Sarah defended Denie. "You know she always comes down first and waits for us."

There were no classes at the Jewish Peretz Shule on Friday, but I too had to help with Sabbath chores. Papa kept his shop open on Friday night and all day Saturday. ("What can we do? This is America, not Chernobyl," he defended his practice to my Bubbie.) But Mamma marked the Sabbath with the traditional preparations.

At noon on Friday the wooden bowl and the chopping-knife lay on the dish tray by the kitchen sink and the house smelled of gefilte fish and chicken soup, herbs and black pepper, of sweet carrot tzimmes and of winey prune and raisin compote.

Denie and I had our special jobs. Mine were to polish Mamma's tall silver candlesticks for the blessing of the Sabbath lights, to lay the dining-room table with white linen, to set out the "good" dishes and the Community Plate, and to shine the outside brass door handle and doorbell "like shining gold". Denie's job was to cut up enough newspaper -- in the absence of tissue that oranges came wrapped in -- so that one need not tear paper for toilet use on the Sabbath.

Denie, who was in Grade One, should have been waiting for me in the basement. But she was not there. I shouted her name in the girls' washroom but my voice only echoed the emptiness of the late afternoon.

"Better go up to her class and see if she has to stay in or something. It's nearly a quarter to four," Bessie urged. "My mother'll kill me if I'm late home Friday."

The door to Denie's classroom was locked. Miss Brooke also liked to leave early on Fridays.

"Maybe Denie is waiting for us outside. It's a suchy nice day," Sarah offered.

But Denie was not there.

"Go to the office. Maybe the teacher punished her and she has to stay in on the line." Bessie always saw a cloud. Sarah and I looked at each other. Denie in the office for misconduct? Hardly possible. Nevertheless, I ran to verify and returned with the ambivalent gratification of knowing that my Denie was not there. "You see, Bessie?"

We went out into the street again. "She knows she can't cross the streetcar tracks herself," I began to worry. "And I know she won't go home without me!"

The large clock above the school door, the one with the Roman numerals and the wire mask, said four. Perhaps for some reason Denie did go home with someone else.

✡ ✡ ✡

My voice preceded me as I entered the door. "Ma, is Denie home?"

"No, Sophela. She's not with you?" Mamma came to greet me with concern.

"I looked for her everywhere in school and outside and she's not there. I thought maybe she came home with someone else."

"No." Mamma began to look worried. "Where can she be? Soon it'll be dark outside and we have to light the candles. Maybe she went to her friend's house?"

"Denie wouldn't go alone after school. She knows she has to wait for me. And today is Friday yet."

"Maybe she went to Papa's store," Mamma suggested. She was glad to find a reason to pull Papa into the emergency. "Philip," she said over the phone, "Denie didn't come home with Sophie. Is she by you? No? All right. I'll phone. Yeh, I'll let you know."

But Denie was not at our auntie's house; neither was she at her friend Ruthie's. As a matter of fact, Ruthie's mother was in distress too, for Ruthie was not home yet either.

The dining-room clock chimed four forty-five. Mamma phoned Papa again. "Philip, what shall we do? It never happened before. The children always come home together ...." I heard the familiar tremor which signified incipient hysteria. "You think so?" Mamma continued. "All right. Call the police. Call me back."

We waited patiently.

Just as the phone rang again, the door opened. Denie walked in. She was smiling as she sang gaily,

Jesus loves me, yes I know
For the Bible tells me so ....

"Denie, where were you!" Mamma shouted, lifting the receiver. And to Papa, "She's here! She just came in! Why didn't you wait for your sister? You know you have to ... Philip, it's all right. I'll call you back." Mamma replaced the receiver as Denie's face prepared itself for tears.

"I was waiting for you outside school," she whimpered, "with Ruthie and a few more girls. And a lady came over and said, 'Little girls, you want to learn sewing?' And Ruthie said, 'Yes,' and I said, 'I have to wait for my sister'." Denie ran on and on. "And the lady said, 'You come with me and we'll phone your mother from my house.' And I forgot to remind her!" Denie dissolved into tears.

Mamma and I were horrified. "You went with a stranger? How many times have I told you you shouldn't go with anyone!" Mamma was shouting. "Woe is me! What could happen to a child in a big city? How many times did I tell you you should not go with ...." I shuddered. Mamma had told us so many weird stories, and read so many tales of warning from The Forward.

"You said we shouldn't take candy -- and we shouldn't go with a man! This was a nice lady!"

"Lady -- man -- makes no difference!" Mamma was wringing her hands. "Nu, tell me -- so where did she take you? What did you do there?"

"She took us by the big house on the corner near the school and she showed us sewing." Denie took a piece of cotton and a threaded needle from her pocket. "See? With this pink 'broidery thread."

"What else did you do?" Mamma tried to control her voice as she looked at the innocuous fabric and thread with suspicion.

"She learned us a new song," Denie smiled through her blurred eyes.

    Jesus loves me, yes I know

she began again in her sweet slightly off-pitch voice.
    The doorbell rang just as Mamma was about to detonate one of her famous maledictions. I ran to the door. A big policeman in uniform filled the doorway.
    "It's about the missing child, Ma'am," he called to Mamma. He spoke with a proper burr.
    "She's home! She's home already!" Mamma and I spoke together. "She just came in, Mr. Policeman. Thank you very much!" Mamma put a protective arm around the trembling Denie.
    "Where were you, little girl?" the policeman asked. "Your mother was worried about you."
    "I -- I went singing and sewing." Denie hardly dared to look up.
    "Singing and sewing? Where?"
    "By the lady's house -- the big house on the corner ...."
    The telephone interrupted and I heard Mamma whisper, "Yes, Philip, it's all right. The police is here now. I'll call you back."
    The policeman said, "The big house? Oh, you mean the Carter house. The Missionaries! What do you know about that!"
    "Missionern!" Mamma exploded in Yiddish. "All my black dreams on their heads! This we need yet! Singing and sewing! Some sewing! 'Jesus loves me' they sing! And a mother goes crazy at home!" She was biting the end of her handkerchief to contain herself. "And here is the Golden Land already. Here they try to steal our children! We didn't have enough in Russia?"
    "Don't worry, Ma'am. Just tell your child not to go with strangers again. We'll have a look in on Mr. Carter. We know him and his crew.
    "They sure like to start their sowing early. Good-day, Ma'am."
    As he left we stood numbly facing each other. Denie didn't know what was expected of her. Mamma turned to the phone to call Papa again.
    "Come, Denie," I said, "let's go polish the candlesticks. Soon Mamma has to light the candles for Shabess."

Shekspir was Jewis

The road home from Strathearn School seemed longer than usual that dull November afternoon. It was already after four o'clock and Mamma would be worried. But not half so worried as when I would tell her what had happened in school that afternoon.

No need to ask if Mamma was at home. Mamma had to rest a lot and we had to be good children and not aggravate her.

As I turned the doorknob I heard her voice.

"So late you're from school?"

"I had to help the teacher correct spelling books." Mamma and I considered this an honour.

"Nice," said Mamma. "You going to Shule now?"

"Yes, Mamma. But first I have to do my homework for Lerem Sherr."

"First eat something," Mamma offered. "The bread man brought fresh kimmel bread. Don't forget to shake up the milk or you'll take off all the cream."

"Don't worry, Mamma. I'll do it."

I entered the dining room and laid my books on the massive oak table. I was not at ease.

It was hard to stay after school with such turmoil in my heart, even to help the teacher. Now I had to hurry or I'd be late.

As I bit into the great buttered oval of crusty bread fragrant with Mamma's luscious plum jam, I was tense. Surely I couldn't break this news to Mamma. If only it had happened in the morning. Then I could have discussed it at noon with Papa when he came home for lunch; but it had happened in the afternoon, and he worked late every night in his tailor shop on Main Street.

The sideboard facing me held the secret of my distress. It was made of polished oak, like the round table and high-backed leather-seated chairs, its lower section a china cabinet with brass-knobbed leaded glass doors. Instead of holding our new set of porcelain dishes, our china cabinet held books. Papa, a self-taught man, loved books, and just as Mamma saved her pennies to pay Mr. Popper, the peddler, fifty cents a week until the china was paid for, Papa spent his pin money on books. The books stood in two rows, one behind the other, in their colourful cloth bindings, some singly, others in sets of two or more. The newest acquisitions always had the place of honour up front.

"Books are teachers," Papa said, "and you have to give them a place of honour in your home."

Thus it was that I first became acquainted with the names of Tolstoy, Pushkin, Chekhov, Dostoyevsky, and with our own Yiddish classicists: Mendele, Peretz, Sholem Aleichem and -- Shekspir.

The gold letters on the red cloth binding announced proudly in Yiddish: Shylock -- Der Koifman fun Venedig (Shylock, the Merchant of Venice) fun Villiam Shekspir. How was I to know that Shakespeare wasn't a Jew? Had I ever heard his name anywhere else than at home or in any language other than Yiddish?

So, when our Grade Four teacher had told us that afternoon in the English public school that she was going to read us "a tale from Shakespeare", I raised my hand.

"Please, Miss, we have him at home in the china cabinet."

"In the china cabinet?" she had repeated in amazement, her lovely British accent trailing into the halls of Strathearn School. "What -- I mean whom?"

"Shekspir!" I announced proudly.

"Do your parents read English?" she asked with interest.

"They don't have to. Shekspir writes in Yiddish. He's Jewis so he writes in Yiddish."

Miss Cranshaw was aghast.

"Who told you this?" she asked.

"Nobody." I was mistress of the situation. "My father buys his books. We keep him in our new china cabinet where we keep all the books."

"In Yiddish?" Miss Cranshaw asked again. "You're sure it's Shakespeare?"

"Sure I'm sure! The book is about Shylock, a Jew who ...."

"Of course!" Miss Cranshaw was relieved. "Shakespeare did write a book about a Jew called Shylock. But Shakespeare was an Englishman -- perhaps the greatest Englishman who ever lived. And he wrote in English, more than 300 years ago, in beautiful poetry. In English!"

The children laughed. All but three of the thirty-six were Jews. They became self-conscious. They laughed.

My eyes filled with tears. What was going on here? Why were they laughing? Surely they knew I was telling the truth!

"The whole book is in Yiddish!" I insisted.

"Well, Shylock was hardly a Jew to be proud of," said Miss Cranshaw coldly. "Why would your father want that book on his shelf?"

How could I break this news to Mamma? What could I tell her? If only Papa had been home!

As I struggled with my Yiddish homework, I decided to spare her. I'd speak to my Jewish teacher. Surely she'd help me right this slander!

I ran all the way to Shule. I caught my teacher just as she was about to enter the classroom.

"Lerern Sherr," I gasped in Yiddish, "I must ask you something."

"Yes, Shulamis." She called me by my Jewish name.

"I told my teacher in school today that Shekspir is Jewish and he writes in Yiddish ...."

Lerern Sherr's pretty face suggested a smile.

"She says he's not a Jew! She says he's an Englishman and he lived more than 300 years ago!" I trembled with indignation.

Miss Sherr put her arm around my shoulder.

"Don't cry," she consoled me softly. "William Shakespeare *was* an Englishman." She spoke his name as it is spoken in English. "And he did write in English more than 300 years ago."

"So why is he in our china cabinet in Yiddish?" I pleaded.

"Because Shakespeare was a great man with a great heart and a great talent," she answered gently. "He now belongs to the whole world. We read him in Yiddish because he is translated into Yiddish. And into many other languages. Because Jews and other people want to know what Shakespeare has to say."

"And Shylock -- what's wrong with Shylock?" I sobbed. "She says we can't be proud of Shylock and my father shouldn't keep him on the shelf!"

"Come into the classroom, Shulamis. Come. We will talk about it in class." She ushered me through the open door.

Slowly, slowly the world spread out before me, but it would be a long time before I felt at home in that world outside my father's house.

וויליאם שעקספיער

William Shakespeare (or as the Yiddish under the picture says it: Villiam Shekspir) -- the frontispiece from the all-Yiddish edition of Shakespeare's Famous Works (3rd reprint) published by Druckerman, New York, 1912.

דער קויפמאן פון וועגעדיג.

(שיילאָק)

אין וועגעדיג האָט געוואוינט א איד מיט דעם נאָמען שיי־
לאָק. ער איז געווען א פּראָצענטניק, און ער האָט
געמאכט א גרויסעס פערמעגען לייהענדיג געלד אויף
פּראָצענט צו די דאָרטיגע קריסטען.

שיילאָק האָט ניט איבריג ליעב געהאַט זיינע
קריסטליכע שכנים, און די קריסטען האָבען איהם נאָך
וועניגער געליעבט. איינער פון זיי, א געוויסער אנטאָניא, א יונגער
קויפמאן פון וועגעדיג, האָט איבערהויפט געהאסט שיילאָק׳ן. ווען אנ־
טאניא האָט בעגענגט שיילאָק׳ן אויף דער ריאלטאָ (מאַרק), האָט ער איהם
געזידעלט און בעליידיגט. שיילאָק האָט געשוויגען, אָבער ער האָט דער־
ווייל געפלאנט זיך נוקם צו זיין אן איהם.

אנטאָניא האָט געהאַט א גוטען פריינד, א געוויבען באסאניא.
דיעזער באסאניא איז געווען א וואוילער יונג, א קליינער עושר און ליעב
געהאַט צו לעבען איבער זיינע איינקינפטע. באסאניא האָט דערפאר אפט
בענעטהיגט געלד און אנטאניא האָט איהם אימער געהאָלפען.

איינמאל איז באסאניא געקומען צו אנטאניא׳ן און איהם דערצעהלט
אזא געשיכטע: ער ליעבט שוין זייט לאנג א יונגע און שעהנע דאמע. מיט
א קורצער צייט צוריק איז איהר פאטער געשטאָרבען און איהר איבערגע־
לאזט א גרויס פערמעגען. יעצט וויל ער זיך וועגדען צו דיעזער דאמע און
דאריף ערשיינען ווי עס פאסט וועגיגסטענס פאר א רייכען מאן. ער האָט
אָבער קיין געלד ניט און ער פערלאנגט, אז אנטאניא זאל איהם אויסבאָרגען
די נעטהיגע סומע.

גראדע דאמאַלס האָט אָבער אנטאניא קיין געלד ניט געהאַט. זיין
גאַנצעס פערמעגען איז געווען אריינגעלעגט אין שיפען מיט סחורה וואָס

The first page of The Merchant of Venice from the author's copy of Shakespeare's Famous Works (Druckerman, New York, 1912).

Denie Needs a Tonic

The dining-room clock read 8:15. We had to leave for school. It was winter, and our Denie, who had just recovered from another cold, would return to school this morning after an absence of a whole week. I was a robust girl of ten. Denie was six, a pale, thin little girl, prone to nose colds, sore throat and earaches.

Our mother had spoken to Mr. Schmerling, the druggist, who decided Denie needed a tonic. He especially recommended Scott's Emulsion, a fine blend of cod-liver oil and other good things, a tried and true remedy against the Canadian winter's blast.

The great bottle of white, thick, greasy fluid stood on the buffet of the china cabinet in full view, and every morning after breakfast the war was on.

Mamma fired the first shot.

"Dinyela," she used the diminutive, "take the molshon."

Denie was a child of few words.

"No," she said, turning to get her street clothes from the rack in the hall.

"Dinyele. Tochter," Mamma repeated more persuasively from the doorway, "take the molshon."

"No," repeated Denie, leaning against the door with her right rubber shoe in her hands.

"It's so good -- it smells like ice cream ...," pleaded Mamma.

"It's slippery and it stinks fish!" retorted Denie, shuddering.

"Dinyela, Tochterl," pleaded Mamma again, carrying the heavy Russian tablespoon of white sticky stuff into the hall, "take the molshon so you won't be green and skinny. Do like Mr. Schmerling says so you'll get healthy and strong!"

Denie didn't even raise her voice.

"I just said I won't take it!" She pulled her crocheted tam over her sensitive ears to keep Mamma out.

"Gottinyo!" Mamma called to God for reinforcements. "What shall I do with this child? Pale and skinny like a toothpick, and so cold outside you could catch nyemonya, and she won't even hear!"

"Mamma, we'll be late for school," I interceded. Addressing Denie by her public school name to remind her of the obedience it implied, I added, "Dorothy, take the mulshn. We'll be late for school. Hurry already."

Denie was becoming impatient too. Hugging her winter coat tightly to her, she suddenly howled, "I said I won't take it! It stinks fish!"

Mamma was beside herself.

"Woe is me! Like this you speak to a Mother? Like this you speak of a healthy medicine? Shame on you! Me? If the doctor told me I should eat (you should excuse me) *you-know-what*, I would eat it to become strong and healthy!"

"Take the cod-liver oil, Denie," I pressed again, louder this time. "Take it! Don't be such a baby! Let's go to school already!"

"A dollar and a half a bottle," wailed Mamma, "and she won't take it! What shall I do with it? Throw it out?"

Heaven forbid! In our house nothing possibly useful was thrown out. You never knew when you might need it. As for food, "It's a sin to throw out good food. So many poor children in Russia would lick their fingers ...." This last statement I expected to see any day -- in Mamma's red Russian cross-stitch -- on our kitchen wall.

Denie had no sympathy for the poor children in Russia. She ate what she liked and left the rest.

My conscience was clear. I ate everything. And I looked it.

Silence hung heavily on the air, broken only by the sound of Denie kicking the door with her right rubber-covered shoe. The clock struck 8:30. I pictured the principal, Mr. Kneeland, moving about in the school basement where the lines formed to march upstairs.

"Denie Borodensky! Take it!" I cried. "We'll be late for lines! We'll have to go to the office!"

Denie was now in tears.

"Lemme alone! I don't care!" And sobbing, "I'll never take it in my whole, whole life!"

Mamma finally got the message.

"Stubborn like a Borodiansky Kohen!" she exploded, evoking the stubbornness of Papa and his brethren, descendants of the ancient Temple priests, who were blemished with this trait. "Nu, so what shall we do with the molshon?"

Suddenly she turned to me.

"Sophela, Tochter -- you're a big girl. She's a baby. It's a shame to throw out such a healthy molshon! A dollar and a half a bottle! You take it Tochter. You show her ...."

"Mamma, no!" I cried. "I'm not skinny! I don't get colds!"

"Think of the poor children in Russia!" Mamma pleaded. "Such a pity on them! You mustn't waste. 'Who lives without account dies without a shroud.' "

Mamma's proverbs struck horror in my heart.

"Mamma, don't! I'll take it! I'll take it! I won't let it go to waste!" I clenched my fists and held my breath as the great tablespoon went between my teeth. As I swallowed, shuddering with distaste, Denie opened the door to the street and I heard her twitter in her little-girl voice:

"It's healthy! It tastes like vanilla ice cream. Mr. Schmerling says it's good ...."

For the Love of a Kid

How was Papa to know when he rented that summer cottage in Shawbridge that our neighbours would not be Jews? Our country neighbours were always Jewish; the farmers were French-Canadian. Yet when we arrived that Sunday morning we were faced with the fact that our neighbours were not Jews.

For the first few days Denie and I didn't dare to go near them, but from our balcony we saw a tall slender mother, a stout pot-bellied father, and three children -- two girls and a small boy. All had black hair and swarthy skins. We heard laughter ringing in the country air and the music of a language that had no familiar ring.

As the week wore on we could see that the children on the other balcony were looking our way too. Denie and I decided to risk a half-way meeting.

The girls came to meet us. We smiled at each other.

"Hello," said the older girl. "I'm Lucy. This my sister Isabella."

"I'm Sophie. This my sister Denie."

"How old are you?" asked Lucy.

"I'm ten. Denie is seven."

"Us too!" Lucy spoke zestfully. "I'm ten, Isabella seven."

Denie and Isabella stood and smiled at each other while we big girls continued to explore.

"You go to school?" I asked.

"Yeh, Catholic. Grade Five. You?"

"We're Jewis but we go Prodistunt. Jews go Prodistunt. Strathearn School Grade Five. Denie Grade Two."

"Wanna play school?" Lucy asked. "We have a blackboard and coloured chalk."

"And books -- do you have books, Lucy?"

"Yes. The Sisters gave me a book to read in the country. The name is -- wait, I'll get it."

"Whose sister?" I asked.

"The teacher. The nun. We call her Sister," she called over her shoulder.

She returned with a small cotton-bound white volume, Lives of the Saints.

"What's a Saint?" I asked.

"Saints is God's best friends. We pray to them."

"You pray to people?" I was amazed.

"Sure! Don't you?"

"No. My Grandmother prays to God. She talks to Him when she lights her candles Friday night. And she tells Him everything. And He listens. God -- but not a person!"

"Saints is different. They're people but we pray to them they should talk to God for us. We light a candle for them and they tell God. They're special ...."

"By us everyone is special," I said simply. "Let me see your book."

It was a lovely book, the paper fine and white, illustrated with copies of old etchings. Each double page had the illustration on the left side, the tale of the saint on the right. Those illustrations terrified me, one was more horrifying than the other! I had seen a crucifix in Malo's Candy Store. It had made me very sad. I had also seen the soft French-Canadian face and the bleeding heart of the virgin there, and while I had asked no questions, Bessie had offered, "Dat's der god and his mother. You know she wasn't really married?" But these? St. Lawrence being roasted on a gridiron; St. Stephen being stoned; St. Catherine being broken on a wheel!

"St Peter -- upside-down yet, on a cross!" I exclaimed in disbelief "Wha-what's the matter with them?"

"The bad kings tortured them because they believed in Jesus," Lucy said sadly. "But they didn't care. They gladly died for Jesus!"

"Gosh! Like this? You sure it's true?" I looked into her eyes.

"The Sisters don't tell lies!" she flashed back.

"By us they killed people too, for Jesus," I offered. "But it was different .... My mother says Pogroms -- I dunno what ...." We had never really talked about it at home. "It's funny," I tried to lighten the conversation. "By us, in Montreal, St. Lawrence and St. Catherine is streets!" I began to laugh to cover my confusion.

"Don't laugh!" Lucy's voice rose to a bark. "Never laugh like that, you hear?"

"I didn't mean ...," I said. "Let's talk about something else." We pledged a silent agreement that such talk was forever taboo.

The summer wore on gently. Mamma and Lucy's mother became friendly. Both ladies had histories of illness they liked to recount -- a bond which overrode any national or religious barriers. They first visited together at the fruit man's wagon that came by twice a week, and later they invited each other for an occasional cup of tea. It was a fine summer with little rain to keep us indoors. All was well.

✡ ✡ ✡

One Thursday afternoon, as we were having our milk and chocolate biscuits, a small truck drove up the dusty path to Lucy's house.

"A truck?" Mamma commented. "That's funny ...."

"Can't be the butcher," I offered, looking to the kitchen where Mamma's Sabbath chicken and meat were salting on their special board. ("That's to take out the blood and salt their meat before cooking. Only a Shokher has a right to kill, to let blood. And first he has to study for years, like a Rabbi. So we soak and salt to take out blood what's left.")

"I think I saw a goat in the back," offered Denie.

"A goat? Who needs a goat here in the country?" I responded.

It was a goat -- rather, a kid with tiny horns and soft black and white flecked shiny hide. As we watched from afar, we saw Lucy's father and her uncle unload the animal. The uncle was a frequent weekend visitor. I was afraid of his big protruding pouch and his short stubby fingers.

"Sophie, come see!" Lucy called. "Come see the goat!"

Tied by a long tether to the clothesline post behind the house, the frightened creature was jumping about, leaving a trail of black turds behind her.

"Come, Denie," cried the other two children. "Come see how she makes!"

I liked Lucy's mother. I had never met anyone like her. I especially liked her very black eyes and soft guttural laugh, her rich voice and the quick movements of her long fingers. Even her strange speech was pleasing to me.

We greeted her shyly.

"Come closer, children." She fluttered her eyes at us and I wondered whether or not she had touched them up with that little black wooden sword Lucy had once shown me on her mother's dressing table. "It's for her eyes," she had said. "We mustn't touch it. My mother uses it to make her eyes black and shiny. And that's for her cheeks," she had added, pointing to an elegant lidded ivory box.

To me that had seemed like black magic. Nothing touched our Mamma's face but soap and water. Papa didn't approve of such things.

"Here, Ali Baba!" cried the little brother, jumping in front of the timorous animal. "Here, Ali Baba!"

"You can't call a girl goat Ali Baba!" shouted Lucy. But the grownups laughed and the name Ali Baba stuck. Ali Baba grew accustomed to us children and lived the life of Riley, keeping the grass in the back yard clipped and trim with her nibbling and enjoying the leftovers from both our tables. We paid our daily visit to Ali Baba, enjoyed the soft smooth feel of her pelt, and the quickness with which she scampered about, kicking up her white-hoofed hind legs. Her fame reached the neighbouring clusters of cottages and children began to come by to view the pet. One boy delighted us with a song he'd learned at Scouts. It was called Old Hiram's Goat. It told of a goat which ate the clothes off the clothesline, then stood on the train tracks, doomed to die, but,

> He coughed and coughed
> in mortal pain --
> coughed up the shirts
> and flagged the train!

We roared as we considered the unlikelihood of that ever happening, but the boy swore it was true. "Goats can even eat tin cans!" he insisted.

As the weeks wore on, Ali Baba grew fat with the good life. Denie and I grew very fond of her. "I think we love her even more than Lucy's family," she said one night. "They don't pet her like we do. I'll be lonesome for Ali Baba when we go home!"

"Yeh," I confessed, "I like her too ... but when we go home we'll have our own friends and school -- and I think it will be O.K." Denie nodded, but I could see she wasn't too certain. As a matter of fact, I felt she was rather amazed at my callousness.

Two Sundays before Labour Day, Lucy came rushing over to our balcony. "We're having a family party next Sunday!" she exulted. "Like we have end of every summer! The whole family will be here -- all the aunties and uncles and cousins and lots of friends!"

"That's nice," I responded and Denie added, "You're lucky ...."

On Tuesday she came running again. "My mother is making the good things! Come see how good it smells!"

The fragrance of molten honey floated through their screen door. "Nuts too," Lucy offered, "and halvah and Turkish delight my mother puts in. Mmmmm -- so good! And the aunties will bring good things too!"

I envied Lucy the excitement she was experiencing. I knew what great fun family get-togethers could be. We would meet at my Bubbie's house -- aunties, uncles, cousins, friends. How good it was in the basement dining room around the great oval table under the light of the stained-glass Tiffany lamp, its bead fringes swaying gently and the silver samovar gleaming among the tall glasses for tea. Such good things Bubbie always had for us! Nobody had to bring anything. Bubbie always had enough for everyone.

What would Lucy's family party be like?

"Where will so many people sit?" Denie wanted to know.

"Out there on the grass. They'll put up big tables and benches -- from the city ...."

Denie understood. "Oh," she reminisced, "like by our auntie's wedding ...."

Early Sunday morning the cars began to arrive. By noon eight cars had assembled. The yard was full of joyous greetings and the babble of celebration. Even from our balcony we could see the stream of packages, platters of cake and cases of wine, beer and soft drinks being lifted onto the grass for cooling in large tin washtubs filled with large cakes of ice.

Lucy was dressed in her pink frilly party dress when she came to our house. Her hair was shiny from long brushing and the large pink bows were clasped to her hair with pretty brass butterflies.

"My mother invites you all to the feast," she announced.

Mamma excused herself, "on account of a headache," but she urged Denie and me to go. "Go, go. See how they do by other people." So we went.

Together with the other children we helped set up the benches. We brought out plates, napkins and cutlery, so the aunties could set the tables. The big boys were busy digging a trench at the side. When I asked Lucy what it was for, she said, "It's to cook the meat." We smiled in appreciation.

Suddenly there was a loud shout. It was Lucy's uncle. "Come," cried Lucy. "Now it's time! Come in back of the house! It's there!"

Everyone gathered in a great circle around the uncle. Over at the side I could see the post to which Ali Baba was kept tethered. Denie waved lovingly to her from afar. The little goat was leisurely cropping the grass. The uncle said something in that other language. Everyone applauded. Excitement ran high.

While everyone watched, Lucy's uncle led Ali Baba into the centre of the circle. He put his left arm around the nanny goat's neck as if to embrace her. Suddenly his right hand flashed a large knife and before we could realize what was happening, there was a bright stream of blood on the black and white coat of Ali Baba. Her eyes bulged in horror. She hadn't even had time to cry out! Her thin legs buckled and she fell.

The guests applauded. Some called out special words.

Denie and I were stunned. We just couldn't believe our eyes. How could they? And Lucy and her family -- hadn't they known? Our beloved Ali Baba! Their beloved Ali Baba! Why?

Denie pressed her head toward me and began to cry. I put my arms around her and we turned toward home. I could hear the fire crackling and Lucy's words, "It's for the meat."

Against my will I turned in that direction. The uncle and another man were busy flaying the slaughtered animal and cleaning it out for roasting. I covered my eyes.

Lucy came running. "Sophie, taste! This is the best part! You eat it raw!" She offered me a long white quivering filament, the spinal cord of the goat.

My voice came out in a whisper. "How could you, Lucy? She was so nice! Ali Baba was our friend!"

"It's just a goat," she said, turning away. "It's like this every summer -- a goat for the party -- just a goat!" Her voice rose as she spoke.

Denie pulled herself away from me and ran home crying.

"You saw her blood -- and you could eat her? Lucy!" A wave of nausea overtook me. She shrugged her shoulder. I turned away and retched.

Sweet Corn and Bringing Up Children

Twice a week the horse and wagon would stop before our door and our fruit man, Mr. Umansky, would climb the winding stairs, clutching the wrought iron balustrade and ring the doorbell of 128A Colonial Avenue.

"Vichnela," he would call (he had known Mamma in Chernobyl in the old country), "anything today? A good orinch, a grapefruit, a good hef-pek eppl -- femuse, shpies -- onion, potatess, a celery, a kebbitch? A good pickela, maybe?"

Mamma would greet him appreciatively. "Thank you, Mr. Umansky. The femuse smells good?"

"Like a good parfyoom." Mr. Umansky would raise his eyes to the sky. "Like I always say, Vichnela, an eppl should smell from a mile and a fish shouldn't smell from an inch."

"So give me a nice hef-pek femuse, a good celery, a good dozen orinches -- but big ones. A hef-dozen pinanness if you have. Other things I have yet."

On cold days, when he brought the produce into the house, Mamma would suggest, "Maybe a hot glass tea with lemon, Mr. Umansky?"

It was in the autumn, just before High Holidays, that our fruit man would come with the fullness of the harvest.

"Vichnela," he would then call through our open door, "orinches, eppl, Shpies, Rosset, a good McIntosh? A good kentelop -- a mashmelon, pomegrant, grapes -- red, yellow, green seedletz. A good piece vodemelon? All kinds vegetables -- the rose tomatess like good red meat!"

Mamma, refreshed and tanned from her summer in the country, would call back, "Thank you. I'll come take a look myself," and she would join the little circle of women around the back of the wagon. Then as the tired nag waited patiently, the ritual of the senses began: the sniffing of an apple, the tasting of a grape, the tapping of a melon.

Meanwhile, Mr. Umansky would be cutting slivers of red watermelon for the women to sample. "Take. Take. Taste. You'll want more. Such sweetness this year like 'at home' when your teeth were young." And the women would smile and buy.

Melons were my special delight; for Denie it was corn. Denie just couldn't wait for the sweet corn season to arrive. She was a finicky eater -- in keeping with her thin, carrot-topped mercurial body. I ate everything. Denie ate only what she liked and stubbornly refused to be bullied into eating anything she didn't like or more than she wanted. Her favourite abhorrence was soup; her favourite autumn delicacy, sweet corn. That, of all God's bounty, signified harvest for her.

Already during the last weeks in the country, as we padded the farmer's cornfield on our daily walk to the Post Office, Denie had drooled, "See how big they're getting! Can we eat them yet?"

Mamma would reply, "Not yet. When the silky hair will hang down golden, then we'll be able to eat. After Labour Day, Mr. Umansky will bring nice sweet corn."

And Mr. Umansky did.

"Vichnele," we heard him call at noon the first Thursday after our return. "Special visitors today. *Gentleman* corn!" He was referring to the large-kernelled ears, the thick golden variety, the kind we loved to shell into paper cornucopias and munch on our way to school. I smiled at Denie and continued to eat, but Denie dropped her fork and ran to the door.

"Hallo, Roytinka" (Rusty), he greeted her, chucking her under the chin. "You got a new freckle in the country, eh?"

Denie smiled. "You got sweet corn today?" she asked, awaiting the pleasure of hearing the news again. "Yummy."

"Give me four nice big ones," Mamma requested, "for Sunday dinner."

Denie beamed. "I'll bring them up," she offered, her small feet rattling down the stairs before the man.

Sunday dinner was a special time for us, for while Mamma prepared all the traditional delicacies for the Sabbath, Sunday was the time Papa was home, the time we could have a pleasant leisurely meal together in the dining room.

A festive air prevailed as Denie and I set the table in the dining room. The porcelain dishes were on the white cloth, the titillating aroma of roast flanken with prunes and potatoes was in the air and the promise of the traces of yellow cornsilk were in the sink where we had husked the corn for Mamma. What more could we ask for? We beamed at each other in anticipation.

"Mamma," Denie asked, "the big pot on the stove is for the sweet corn?"

"The big pot on the stove is soup -- bean and barley, like always."

A heavy cloud fell over Denie's face. "Yukh!" she exploded, "soup! I won't eat it!" Papa and Mamma exchanged glances. Mamma shook her head.

We washed our hands and took our Sunday places at the round oak table. Papa was in fine spirits. "Mamma made a good dinner today," he offered.

"Yeh," beamed Denie, "sweet corn!"

Mamma entered the dining room carrying the tureen of steaming soup and a ladle. As Papa began to measure out the soup, Denie announced in her little singsong voice, "No soup for me-eeee."

Papa was a mild-mannered man, but if ever he decided to assert himself he was adamant. He remembered a heavy-handed father, so his own philosophy of child-rearing was one of gentle persuasion. Yet he insisted on discipline. Because he had known privation in his youth, he knew the value of food. Today he decided to assert himself.

"Eat a little bit," he coaxed. "It's good for you."

"No soup for me ...," Denie repeated a little less gaily.

Without even raising his eyes, he placed the large rimmed plate before her. "Eat," he said.

Denie didn't say a word. She sat for a moment looking down at her hands, then glanced up at Papa from the corner of her eye.

"No soup -- no sweet corn," said Papa suddenly.

Mamma and I were horrified. Such a treat, so much anticipation, and now? The moment hung heavily in the air as we watched Papa dip the soup into his plate and begin to eat. Denie didn't budge.

"Eat, children," Mamma invited, pretending not to notice. The heavy Russian nickel-silver spoon felt even heavier as I lifted it to my lips. I loved Mamma's rich thick bean and barley soup and Mamma always reminded us that Dr. Ship said it was good for us.

"Eat, Denie," I urged, a sense of desperation rising within me. "After the meat is sweet corn ...."

Zaida and cousin Chaim fishing, circa 1928.

Denie, age 2, 1919.

Denie age 4, Shulamis (Sophie) age 8 with Mamma and Papa, 1921.

Shulamis, 10 weeks old, 1913.

From left: Bubbie Yelin (mother of Shulamis' husband), Shulamis holding daughter Gilah, 10 weeks, Mamma, Bubbie, 1944.

Papa and Mamma with Shulamis
and Denie, Val David, 1926.

Papa, Mamma, Shulamis, Denie
with cousin Sonja, 1926.

Bubbie with Denie, 1926.

Denie and Shulamis on Mt. Royal, 1929.

Shulamis at launching of book of poems, Seeded in Sinai, 1975.

Shulamis and friends at summer camp, Saranac Lake, New York, 1933.

Shulamis in front of 28A Colonial Avenue (house on right with awning), her childhood home, in November 1983, upon publication of first edition of Shulamis.

Dover's Grocery on Prince Arthur Street

The corner of St. Catherine Street and St. Lawrence Boulevard circa 1910. (Notman Photographic Archives)

Prince Arthur and Cadieux Streets. Cadieux became de Bullion in 1927. On the northwest corner is Malo's candy shop. Diagonally across from it on the south side of Prince Arthur is Dover's Grocery. (Notman Photographic Archives)

The Monument National Theatre on St. Lawrence Boulevard -- The Main -- as it looked in the 1940's. (Notman Photographic Archives)

A postcard view of the CPR station at Belisle's Mills, (Notman Photographic Archives).

Row 4: Shulamis (Miss Borodensky); Woodblocks -- Dr. Alex Schwortzman, Prof. Abraham Rotstein (University of Toronto); Cymbals -- Jack Greenberg; Rattles -- Dr. Claire Mendelsohn Friefeld (nutritionist), Dr. Danny Silver (psychiatrist). Row 3: Tambourines -- Barney Pollack (lawyer), ?; Triagles -- Dr. Leah Paltiel Schnitzer, Fanny Glassman (teacher in Israel); Bells -- Janet Ruskin Avrith, ?. ?, Leah Eisner, ?. Row 2: Drum -- Leo Kolber (TD Bank, Cemp Investments), rest of row unknown except for Dr. Israel Libman (white shirt, far right).. Row 1: Names of children unknown. These children came from two Grade Two classes, my own and that of Miss Clarice Geller. I wish I knew all their names and where they are today. Shulamis brought the idea of a rhythm band with her to Bancroft School from the Peretz Shule where it was introduced by principal Jacob Zipper.

Shulamis Yelin, 1989.

But Denie just sat, her head stubbornly bent forward, her lips firmly set. "No," she muttered softly but definitely.

"No soup -- no sweet corn," repeated Papa.

I didn't dare look up. I knew Denie would rather die now than give in. I kicked her under the table and continued to spoon my soup into my mouth.

Papa, Mamma and I had finished our soup, but Denie had not touched hers.

It was now not only a contest of wills; it was a test of love. Mamma looked at Papa. All the fun had gone out of the room. Papa pretended not to notice. "What's next?" he asked. "The soup was delicious, Vichna."

Mamma bit her lip and rose to collect the plates.

"Leave Denie's plate," Papa said. Mamma did not dare to contradict. Even the savoury meat dish Mamma brought into the room could not dispel the dolor of the moment. Papa again apportioned the food. We ate in silence. Denie pushed her soup plate away and began to peck at the meat Mamma had placed before her. She was unable to enjoy its goodness; she was too proud to cry.

I held my breath as Mamma went into the kitchen to bring in the corn. There they lay -- long and golden, plump and perfectly formed "gentlemen" on the white china platter, just begging to be picked up and enjoyed. Papa took one up and began to eat. Mamma offered me mine. When Denie stretched out her hand to take her ear of corn, Papa quietly but firmly again repeated, "No soup -- no sweet corn."

It seemed to me the chandelier had begun to sway. Denie withdrew her hand and tightened her lips. Papa finished his ear of corn and turned to Denie. "Well?" he asked.

"No," she retorted angrily. "I don't care! I won't eat it!"

"Very well then," said Papa, picking up her portion and bringing it to his lips. "Then I'll have that corn." And he did.

I just couldn't believe my eyes. Neither could Denie. With a burst of tears, she fled into our bedroom shouting, "I hate him! I hate him!"

I was stunned.

"Whom? What were you saying?" Mamma called after her.

"I -- I hate -- Mr. Umansky!" she shouted as she banged the door shut.

Mamma stood in the hall between the dining room and our bedroom glowering at Papa.

"Tatitchko!" she exploded in anguish, using the Russian epithet. "Just like her father -- a stubborn Borodiansky!"

I went into the kitchen and began to wash the plates.

די אמעריקאן
פוירניטשור קא.

4436 סט. לארענס בולווארד

עטלאכע טירן נידריקער פון
מאונט ראיאל

מיט א פולן אויסוואל פון:

דיינינג-רום, בעד-רום און
טשעסטערפילד סעטס

אלע פון די לעצטע סטיילס
צו די ביליגסטע פרייזן

The American Furniture Co.
4436 ST. LAWRENCE BLVD.

דיזער פלאץ איז באיגעשטיערט גע-
וארן פון קענעדיען טשואינג
גאם קא. לימיטעד

מאנופעקטשורערס פון

טשיקלעטס

מיר דאנקען אלע געשעפטסלייט וואס האבן אנאנסירט אין אונזער זשורנאל

From *Yiddishe Kinder* (1927). The large bold Yiddish letters in the bottom ad is a literal rendition of 'Chiclets' chewing gum.

I Take Scripture

Early in the term Miss Swan read a notice from "the office" stating that Jewish parents had the option of withdrawing their children from the study of the New Testament if such study was against their principles or beliefs.

Our Grade Five had been dismissed for lunch -- we called it dinner -- and we were deep in discussion on our way home. Should we or shouldn't we take Scripture?

As usual, Bessie's was the voice of authority. "I'm sure my father won't let me listen to that Jesus business. Huh! All about Yoshka (Jesus)! Who needs him anyway? You know he was Jewish? Some Jew!"

Sarah, from her anarchist father's home, spoke softly, "My father says it's poison. All kinds religions is poison. In America you don't need God, you don't need Jesus. It's not like in Russia ...."

"In Russia they make you a goy ride-away. The priest makes Jewis children a goy first chance!" Bessie abetted.

"It's good we go to the Prodistunt School," I intervened. "No priests. Just Scripture -- if you want."

"But I don't have to take it!" Bessie proclaimed virtuously. "Why should I? We have the Torah!"

Around the tiny kitchen "table" -- a board which covered the washtub -- we sat at dinner. Mamma served the zharkoya, her name for pot roast.

"I like the crispy part," I put in my bid.

"Give Denie with juice," Papa reminded. Denie smiled in appreciation. We waited for Mamma to sit down before we began to eat.

"The teacher said we should ask if we could take Scripture," I said.

"What's Scripture?" Mamma wanted to know.

"Scripture is about Jesus. First thing in the morning. Twenty minutes in back of the room. The English have to take it. The Jews can choose."

"All my black dreams on their heads," Mamma cursed. "We didn't have enough with the pogroms in Russia?"

"Take. Take Scripture," said Papa quietly.

"Philip, you know what you're saying?" Mamma was aghast.

"I said, 'Take Scripture'," Papa repeated. "Here is Canada, not Russia. Here a person has to know everything."

"Ma?" I questioned timorously.

Mamma smiled vaguely. Feelings were her department. For logic in America she bowed to Papa. Nevertheless, she exploded. "What do you want from the child?"

Papa was silent. She turned to me.

"And you? What do you want?" she asked.

"Me?" I replied without looking up. "Me? I like to know the stories. It's nice. The teacher takes you in the corner, back of the room by the window, and she sits on a desk with her feet on the seat and she tells from her big black Bible. And the children who don't take have to do arifmetic," I added menacingly.

"Only the goyim take?" Mamma asked again.

"Only the goyim and the Jews that want."

"How many take altogether?"

"With me will be five: John and Thomas and Walter, and me and the scholarship girl, Annie Rosen. She needs it for scholarship. Her father has the grocery store on Pine."

"Philip," Mamma trembled. "What do we need it for? With the shkotsim?"

"Vichna, it won't hurt her. She goes to Jewish school -- she learns about Jews. Let her know this too."

In the morning Miss Swan invited the Scripture-takers to the back of the room by the window. Bessie glared at me over her shoulder. Sarah too was surprised. Annie Rosen they understood. She needed it for her Scholarship. But I?

I revelled in the beauty of the King James translation as we listened to the rolling rhythms of The Good Samaritan spoken softly and lovingly by Miss Swan:

And a certain man went down from Jerusalem to Jericho and he fell among thieves which stripped him of his raiment and wounded him and departed, leaving him half dead. And by chance there came down a certain priest that way. And when he saw him, he passed by on the other side ....

"Hmmm, waddya expect from a priest?" Bessie reacted when I reported to my friends on my way home to lunch what I had been learning. "A priest is a Catholic, a French ... so what happened next?" Bessie's judgments were consistent.

I continued to quote:

And likewise a Levite, when he was at the place looked on him and passed by on the other side.

"A Levite?" Bessie asked again. "Must be a mistake. What's a Levite?"

"Maybe she means Levy?" Sarah offered.

"No," I replied devoutly, "a Levite. The teacher said a few times: a Levite .... She didn't say what it means."

"So who helped him, that poor man? What happened next?" Bessie couldn't wait.

"A certain Samaritan!" I announced triumphantly ... "a good Samaritan helped him." I quoted again:

But a certain Samaritan as he journeyed, came where he was and he had compassion on him, and went to him and bound up his wounds, poured in oil and wine, and set him on his own beast and brought him to an inn and took care of him. And on the morrow when he departed, he took out two pence and gave them to the host and said unto him, "Take care of him, and whatsoever more thou spendest, when I come again, I will repay thee."

"Must be Jewis," Bessie had no doubts. "Must be Jewis," she repeated armed with proof. "Washed his wounds with wine -- like for Kiddush. By Jews is wine. Not whisky. By our Mrs. Quinn, next door, is only whisky, not wine."

We pondered the story silently the rest of the way home.

At the table, Papa again asked, "What did you learn today?"

"I took Scripture," I beamed.

"What did you learn in Scripture?"

"It's a story about a priest and a Levite and a Good Samaritan," I offered in much the same way as I told my jokes about an Englishman, a Frenchman and a Jew.

Now it was Mamma's turn. "A priest and a Levite?"

"A Kohen and a Levi, from the Temple," Papa explained in Yiddish. "In English it's a Priest and a Levite."

"Papa, what's a Samaritan?" I took the opportunity to ask.

"A Samaritan is a man from Samaria," Papa explained.

I was stunned. "Papa, a Kohen, a Levi, from the Temple! And they didn't stop to help?"

"You see?" Mamma was beside herself. "You see what you're doing to the child?"

Papa wasn't listening. "Shulamis," he said slowly, looking directly into my eyes, "there are good people and bad people everywhere. You have to choose what you will be. It's the same in all lands, in all religions. That's why you have to study so you will know. A person mustn't be afraid to know ...."

"Philip, stop it!" Mamma cried in panic. "Let her go to school!"

"In Canada you are free to be a good Jew and a good Canadian -- a good person," Papa continued. "That's why we came to this land, isn't it, Vichna?"

"Philip, stop it!" Mamma cried again. "Sophela, go. Go to school already. You'll be late!" She pushed me to the door. "Here -- take -- two cents for candy!"

The Girl Who Stole Santa Claus

Monday morning.

Chanukah had just passed. We had celebrated at home with candles, latkes and Chanukah gelt for which Papa had made us special little white and blue striped cotton bags. The festivities at Shule -- the decorations, the story-telling, the songs and the special concert -- all had been topped off by the celebration at my Bubbie's house the night before. My ears still rang with the shouts of pleasure as family and friends greeted each other, with Zaida's voice chanting the blessings over the full menorah, the flames of its nine small coloured candles dancing out the Miracle of the Oil. My tongue still tingled with the taste of the thin, hot, yeast-blown pancakes dripping with goose fat and brown molten honey kept warm in a large basin at the edge of the stove.

I licked my lips in pleasant memory as I clutched my little bag of coins we children had been encouraged to collect from the adults. This was Chanukah gelt, commemorating the coin Judah the Maccabbee had struck to mark the victory over the Greeks and the rededicating of the Temple.

Suddenly I realized there were no children on the street. Again I was late for school! I began to run, the blurred edges of the Temple receding into the realities of Prince Arthur Street leading to Strathearn School.

As I charged up the stairs to my classroom, I tucked my private world into my heart, took my seat, and readied myself for the dichotomy which had entered our lives.

After the recital of the Lord's Prayer which everyone, except Bessie, repeated in unison, Miss Cranshaw handed out an arithmetic assignment and we, the five Scripture-takers, went to our accustomed corner in back of the room for our private rendezvous with "the Lord". Christmas was two weeks away and at Strathearn School the windows were blooming with red and green bells, Santas and winter scenes. Our class was making little calendars, Christmas gifts for our parents.

Miss Cranshaw opened her black Bible and read:

And there were in the same country shepherds abiding in the fields keeping watch over their flocks by night. And the Angel of the Lord came upon them and the glory of the Lord shone round about them and they were sore afraid. And the Angel said unto them, "Fear not, for I bring you good tidings of great joy which shall be unto all people. For unto you is born this day in the city of David, a Saviour which is Christ the Lord."

And I together with the three Christian children and Annie, "the scholarship girl", listened carefully to the beautiful melodious rhythms of the King James version of the New Testament, the words inscribing themselves indelibly in my memory. I listened. I enjoyed. Yet somehow, a shrill note was struck within me. The City of David I knew; the Angel of the Lord I recognized. But -- the Saviour which is Christ? Christ the Lord? Unless -- unless, of course, God and Lord were not quite the same ....

"They can have their Lord!" Bessie barked when I told my friends about it at recess.

"I wish we could have Christmas," mourned Sarah. "It's so pretty with a Christmas tree. You saw by Malo's candy store the Christmas tree they put up? And so beautiful decorated with silver streamers and snow and on top with an angel ...."

"That's their 'angel of the Lord'," hissed Bessie. "Ya know, ya shouldn't even go there now. My mother makes me peanut briddle at home."

I was not much disturbed by the Christmas tree at Malo's. It was beautiful and magical, but somewhere in my head there was a fence with a sign on it that read,

Malo's Candy Store corner Cadieux and Prince Arthur is good for candy and scribblers and things, but that's all.

Three women kept the store, tall sad-faced pretty women, a mother and two fading daughters; they spoke only French. They lived on Colonial Avenue near us, behind wooden double doors and blind-drawn windows in the self-contained cottage next to the lane. One rarely saw any movement in or out of those doors. I clearly recall the black crepe and the wreath that had decorated those doors the previous winter as through the silent snow had run the news that Mr. Malo was dead. He had never served us, but I remembered him showing himself occasionally from behind the shiny green curtains at the back of the store. That summer and every summer after that, there bloomed in the tiny garden in front of their house a pretty bush of bleeding hearts, so beautiful, so sad.

After his death, the three ladies dressed in black with a white lace ruffle at the neck; they continued to run the store themselves. No matter how noisy the children were on the street, when we entered Malo's we dropped our voices, and while we took our time choosing and deciding on which best buy to spend our two cents, we spoke politely.

Sarah lived on Cadieux Street, across from Malo's.

When we met after lunch to return together to school, Sarah was again full of the Christmas tree at Malo's.

"They have little white furry Santa Clauses on it too, now, and they were just putting on candles when I was there!" she exulted. "You should see how beautiful it is! I just wish we could have a Christmas tree!"

"Sarah! What are you saying? We just had Chanukah!" I tried to ease her.

"Sure! But what's Chanukah? My mother made me a few latkes and she gave me some Chanukah gelt -- a quarder -- so?"

"Didn't your father light the candles?" I asked again. "And didn't they tell you about the oil -- how it burned eight days instead of one? And about the brave Maccabbees, how Mattathias yelled, 'Who is for the Lord follow me!' And his son Judah, the Hammer, freed the Jews from the Greeks ...." I grew increasingly more excited as I relived the pleasures of the week.

"Sophie, I'm not like you. I don't go to Shule and I don't have a Bubbie here. And my father didn't tell me nothing. He works late in the dress factory -- and they don't believe in it!"

"They don't?" I was distressed.

"They're 'narkistin' (anarchists)," she defended.

"What's 'narkistin'?" I asked.

"I don't know, but I know it's good. They want everybody should be good and should be free -- everybody. But it's not with God and it's not with holidays ...."

"So how do they have fun?" I persisted.

"They talk. They have friends and they come to our house and they make speeches and they talk. They have a lady comes sometimes from New York and her name is Emma Goldman. She talks loud and tells them they have to make the world free. Then they sing songs and drink tea with lemon and sponge cake."

"They didn't tell you about the Maccabbees?" I asked again. Something terrible was happening to the gentle Sarah.

"No," she replied. "My parents want all people should be free and make a good world. Not just Jews. They don't like *no* religion."

I took her hand in mine and we walked silently to school.

Preparations for Christmas took over. Because of fear of possible fire, we had no class tree, but Miss Cranshaw had set up a crèche on the book table at the front of the room. It was made of cardboard and it was painted red and green and had white sparkling snow for a ground. In the centre stood a tiny cradle with the Christ Child in it, a shining halo carefully attached to his pretty head, and Mary and Joseph and the Wise Men knelt before him. On the backdrop oxen and sheep were painted. We sang Silent Night and Away in a Manger and Good King Wenceslas and I rejoiced in the beautiful music as the words drifted into the hall to join with voices of the other classes, composed largely of Jewish children, who were also preparing for Christmas and looking forward to the holiday that would follow.

On Tuesday Sarah brought a ball to school and at recess we played Stando in the basement. We looked ahead to the winter break when we would be free for ten whole days to play outside and go skating and sliding in St. Louis Square.

Three or four days before the holidays, Miss Cranshaw looked up at Sarah and said, "Why so pale, Sarah? You look like you had fallen into a flour barrel." Sarah did not answer. She lowered her eyes and covered her face with her hands. Next day, and until classes broke for the holidays, Sarah did not appear in school. I was sorry she was missing the excitement of the season. Only Bessie couldn't allow herself to enjoy the scene. "Good she's not here. She doesn't have to be here. Every day 'holy, holy'. It's enough already!"

On my way home from our Christmas party, I rang Sarah's bell. Her mother answered.

"How is Sarah?"

"She's better now. She had a very high fever."

"Tonsils?" I asked.

"No, the doctor didn't know what it was. But today she is better. No, don't come in. In a day or two she'll come out to play."

"I brought her the calendar she made in school and the teacher sent her candy, like we all got."

"Thank you, Sophie. I'll give it to her. Thank you."

Every morning when I went out to play I walked by Sarah's house to see if she was out. It was only towards the end of the week that I found her sitting at the top of her stairs huddled in her heavy coat and scarf. She was even paler than I remembered her in school that day. She was feeding the birds bits of white bread.

When she saw me, she tried to turn away.

"Sarah," I called softly from the foot of the iron staircase.

She rose, sending the two sparrows on the banister into flight.

"Sarah, how are you feeling?" I tried again.

"I-I'm a little better," she answered looking away.

"May I come up and talk to you?"

"Come -- but I don't feel good." And suddenly she was weeping into her mittens.

I ran up the stairs. "What hurts you, Sarah?" I wanted to cry too.

"In here." She put her hand on the left side of her chest, then bent over and continued to weep.

"What does the doctor say?"

"He says it's nothing. What does the doctor know! He just gives bitter medicines. And now he says I should go play outside."

"So take your red ball and we'll play."

"I don't have my red ball anymore." She looked up at me and suddenly again broke into tears. "I threw it away."

"Sarah, why? Why did you throw away such a good red ball?"

"It made me sick!" she sobbed. "That rotten ball! It's all on account of that rotten ball!"

I squatted beside her on the stair, and put my arm around her.

"Sarahla," I pleaded, "everybody catches a cold sometimes. So what?"

"No, Sophie. It wasn't just a cold. It wasn't a cold at all." We sat together for what seemed hours as Sarah tried to control her weeping. Finally she looked up. "Sophie, swear. Swear you should drop down dead if you tell anyone!" Her frightened red eyes looked into mine.

"I should -- I should drop down dead!" I uttered, horrified at the thought.

"Swear 'Two fingers up to God'," she looked at me threateningly. "Nobody, you hear? You shouldn't tell nobody! Speshly that -- that Bessie! you hear? Even not your own mother! It's a suchy terrible secret!" She was sobbing again.

Then it poured out.

On the first day of Chanukah, Sarah's mother had given her Chanukah gelt: two new silver dimes and a tiny silver nickel. Sarah had played alone with the money before she went to sleep. She had hoarded it all week as she listened to the other children tell how much they had received from aunts and uncles. With no relatives who celebrated the holiday, Sarah's hoard had not grown.

Each day as she went into Malo's for her two cents worth of candy, she peered around, wondering what she might buy for her precious twenty-five cents. As the excitement over Christmas grew in the school, Sarah decided she would buy that twenty-five cent red rubber ball. Then she could play with the other children and everyone would see how great her Chanukah gelt really was.

I had gone with her to buy the ball.

"Try it," I urged when she paid her money. "Try it. See how high it jumps!"

Sarah was bouncing the ball when Madame Malo suddenly spoke up in a loud clear voice. "Outside!" she ordered.

Sarah was caught unawares. The ball suddenly jumped to an unexpected height and before she could catch it, it bounced on the counter and fell on the floor behind the counter. Madame Malo, who had already moved into the centre of the floor, looked at her severely and said, "Tiens, get it -- get it!"

Sarah went into the magic land behind the counter. Lots of boxes were stacked high upon each other. At the top of the stacks -- she could not believe her own eyes -- lay two open boxes full of little white furry Santa Clauses, the same as adorned the Malo's Christmas tree! The temptation was too great. Sarah grabbed a handful -- two Santas to be exact -- and pushed them into the top of one of her long red woolen overstockings. Madame Malo's impatient voice rose from the side of the store.

"Eh bien, tu as la balle?"

Sarah picked up ball, and with a panicky look, came around the counter. As we walked to school, I said, "Sarah why are you so red? You didn't do nothing wrong. She told you to go get the ball."

Sarah began to run. I ran after her. "Sarah! Sarah! Wait for me!" But Sarah did not stop until she got to the school basement.

The next day, Miss Cranshaw noticed her pallor.

"And I couldn't sleep no more!" wailed poor Sarah, finishing her terrible confession. "I just couldn't sleep at all! Then I began to feel so hot! My mother took my temperature and it was burning! Once I slept and I dreamt she was chasing me, Madame Malo, and yelling, 'Police! Police! Dis terrible girl -- she stoled Santy Claus!' In English yet! Everybody from school was shouting, 'Shame! Shame! Christmas, and she stole Santa Claus!' "

I was too stunned to speak. I sat looking at her, rigid like the icicle that hung from the balcony above.

"Poor Sarah!" I finally uttered.

"Don't 'poor' me!" She jumped up in fury. "It's your fault too! Don't be so innocent! You with your Chanukah, and your family and your Shule! Every day a new story about how much fun you had, and the school with Christmas and the Baby Jesus! I'm Jewish and what do I have? Nothing! A rotten red rubber ball!" I was terrified that her mother might open the door and hear what was going on. That I should be a partner to the crime had never even entered my mind! What could I tell her? How could I comfort her?

Suddenly I had an idea. "Sarah, you know, you could go to Shule too. You don't even have to pay if you can't afford. I'm telling you. Talk to your mother ...."

Sarah clutched my arm. "You swore! You swore to God you won't tell!" she panicked.

"I won't. I promise. I swear again. I just said you should talk to your mother she should write you in Shule. In Peretz Shule it's not so much with God, but it's with stories and songs and holidays. We could go together ...." She looked at me eagerly. Encouraged, I continued, "The teacher could call you Soreh like she calls me Shulamis. Then you could have everything too ...."

There was a long moment of silence, then Sarah rose, rubbed her eyes with her heavy coat-sleeve. We stood looking at each other.

"I have to go in now," she said turning from me.
"You'll tell your mother about Shule?" I pressed again.
"Yes, Sophie, I'll try."
"Soreh," I offered, unwilling to let her go, "you could call me by my Jewish name, Shulamis."
Sarah smiled gratefully. "Thank you, Shulamis."
"Good-bye, Soreh," I kissed her quickly on the cheek and ran down the stairs.

Phone Lancaster 1064 **New York** Glaziers & Picture Framers Mouldings, Pictures, Frames, Trays & Mirrors **GLASS** Plate, Window, Fancy, Tops for Tables, For Automobiles Replaced Mirrors Beveled and Resilvered Picture Framing 3431 ST. LAWRENCE BLVD. Above Sherbrooke.	BE lair 2559 Compliments of **Horn's** CAFETERIA SERVICE The Only Eating Place of its kind 4067 St. Lawrence Boulevard
DR. S. GOLD וויל לאזן וויסן זיינע באקאנטע, אז ער האט אריבערגעצויגן זיין אפיס אין דער ״מעדיקא־דענטאל בילדינג״ (סט. קעטרין — קארנער בישאפ)	
נאראנטי לאאן סינד. אפיס: 4100 קלארק סטריט טעלעפאן, בעלעיר 3356־עם אפן יעדן דינסטיק. און דאנערשטיק אוונט פון 7:30 — 10 אזייגער זונטיק פון 10—12 פרי נאכמיטאג פון 2 — 6 אין פרינץ ארטור האל — האל נומער 3 ווערט א מעמבער אין אונזער סינדיקיים מיר פארקויפן שערס צו $10 א שער מיר פארקויפן קויהלן צו אונזערע מעמבערס אויף א קאאפעראטיוון אופן. מיר דיסקאונטן נאוטס צו אונזערע מעמבערס. שליסט זיך אן אין א סינדיקייט ווי יע־ דער מעמבער ווערט אטענדעט מיט דער בעסטער אויפמערקזאמקייט ביי ארדער. דער באארד אף מענעדזשמענט	Compliments of **Woodhouse & Co.** House Furnishers 79-83 St. Catherine St. W., Montreal

From Yiddishe Kinder, 1927.

Highland Fling

Miss Horner! The name still cleaves the air like the lash of a whip!

Miss Horner, the gym teacher, was little taller than a dwarf. Even as children we knew it. She was strong and wiry with a tightly drawn mouth -- the evil fairy, the black witch of vengeance. Dressed in long black stockings and a short navy tunic, she ruled over the children of the school with a shrill steel whistle which hung from her neck on a black ribbon, and with a long thin wooden rubber-tipped pointer. The fat and the slow suffered most keenly from her, not only from the jolt of the sudden whistle or the flick of the wretched pointer, but also from her scorpion tongue.

It was Miss Horner who brought order into the boisterous basement of the public school and marched up the lines when the principal wasn't there. It was Miss Horner who rounded up the "lates" once the bell had rung, humiliating them for their iniquity and lecturing them on their overriding laziness and shameful ways, setting up for us "glorious examples" upon which to pattern ourselves.

It was winter and for me, the child of an ailing mother, getting ready in the morning was a horror. There was the long woolen underwear to pull on, the long thick stockings to draw up and attach to the bodice garters, the tall black boots to lace, and overstockings, rubbers, and scarves waiting in the hall. Mamma was not there to greet me and offer me breakfast, but an old wizened distant relative of Papa's who lived with us because her children who lived in Cali-Shmendgele (she parodied the golden name of the glorious state of California) had no room for her in their lives. "Ess," she would urge me in the gray 40-watt bleakness of the kitchen as she set a greasy fried egg before me. "Eat and go to school. You'll be late."

But I had no stomach for breakfast or for school. My tongue felt thick and my heavy underwear itched.

Invariably I arrived at school late or just as the bell was ringing. When Miss Horner saw me, I knew my fate was sealed.

"Sophie! You wait outside the door!" she would snap. "I'll see you later!" The exclamation mark in her voice sent a chill through me. Then, with a shrill blow of her whistle, she set the drummer into motion and the lines began to move.

When the basement had been cleared of the last children, I sucked in my breath and waited for the attack.

"Late again," she snapped at me, letting the more fortunate run upstairs as she arranged her less than 4'1" before me in an "at ease" position preparing for the onslaught.

"Late again," she repeated. "You'll never amount to anything if you are always late!" She waited for my defense, but I was now too tense with expectation and fear to speak. "Look at the great women in history!" she continued. "Were they ever late? Laura Secord -- was she ever late?" she demanded, referring to the legendary heroine of the war of 1812-14 between Canada and the United States.

I looked at the minute hand of the Roman-numeralled basement clock behind its iron mask as it moved me inexorably into further lateness.

"Laura Secord. Was she ever late?" she repeated the question to impress it more firmly on my mind. "No! She saved her country! That's what she did. She tied her white lace bonnet tightly under her chin, put on her black Sunday slippers with the silver buckles and, plodding through the mud, she drove her cow -- an excuse, you understand -- to the British Headquarters to warn them that the Rebels were coming! Why, she didn't even stop when one of those precious silver buckles fell off and got lost somewhere in the mud!

"Now," she continued in full wind, "if Laura Secord had got up three minutes too late, or had been even *one* minute late in getting to Headquarters with her cow, what would have happened?"

She waited dramatically once more for my answer.

Caught up in the story, I was still pondering the business of driving a cow. How did one do that? I wondered. I was also torn between the losing of a precious silver shoe buckle and the creeping agony of having to write my name on the board as punishment for lateness again that week.

"Answer me!" she rapped out again, flicking her wooden pointer in the air. "What would have happened if Laura Secord had come one minute late?"

I recalled her reply from previous encounters. "The -- the Rebels would have won the war and we wouldn't belong to the beloved Mother Country any more!"

We were not yet studying history. To me, Laura Secord was a lady who made very delicious chocolate. Her picture was on the boxes which Papa brought to the country every weekend in summer. Nor did I know who the Rebels were. I did understand that a victory of "the rebels" was a fate worse than coming late for school.

"Yes indeed! And we would now be slaves of the United States -- like those Negroes in the South -- instead of being proud subjects of the beloved Mother Country!"

I had never head of "the Negroes in the South". My own relatives lived in the United States and considered themselves, Jews though they were, the freest people in the world, whose sons -- Do you hear, Czar Nicolai? -- might even one day become President!

What was Laura Secord to me anyhow? My own heroine of the moment was The Little Match Girl whose sad story Miss Ransom had recently read us. The little girl had a sick mother and they were so poor! The girl had to sell matches on the London streets to earn a few pennies for bread. But no one cared. On Christmas Eve, when all the people were rejoicing on their way to church, the Little Match Girl froze to death on a London street, her outstretched hand still holding the matches. And no one cared. She was so alone! She died trying to help her poor sick mother!

How I wept into my fists as the teacher read the story. I asked her to read it again and again wept.

But the lady on the chocolate box?

The alternate lashing was with "dear gentle Florence Nightingale who gave herself freely to the noble British soldiers in that Barbaric War with the Dastardly Russians! Gentle noble Florence who went from one man's bed to the next in the night, with only a lantern to light her way!" Miss Horner's eyes took on a faraway look.

"Was *she* ever late? No!" she responded valiantly herself. "No indeed! She knew how eagerly they waited for her, each man thrilling as her shadow came closer to his bed in the dark!"

Dear Papa's dream was for me to "become a nurse, help sick people, be an independent woman and be able to travel anywhere in the world!" With Mamma ailing and Miss Horner lecturing me about "noble Florence Nightingale", I had had enough of nursing by the time I was ten.

When I came into the classroom, the children had already said their morning prayers and sung God Save our Gray (God Save our Gracious King). Miss Ransom, who well knew the ways of Miss Horner, didn't even turn as I moved wretchedly into the room. She just motioned me to put another X by my name on the late list and continued the lesson. The locker monitor now had a chance to get up and move about a bit as he unlocked and locked the lockers with the special key.

"She got you again, eh Sophie?" he grinned. "So why *are* you always late?"

✡ ✡ ✡

The news soon spread that Miss Horner was planning her Annual Spring Gymnastics Exhibition. All classes would participate. All grades would march and do various drills appropriate to their level, but some children would be selected for Special Events like tumbling, ladder exercises, rope climbing and parallel bars. There would also be Folk Dances of the British Isles by groups of children from the various grades.

How I longed to be chosen. I had just participated in the Chanukah Concert at Shule where I had played the heroic Hannah who sacrificed her seven sons rather than let them bow down to the Greek idols or even to kiss the King's ring. How I had gloried in her courage!

"She picked you?" Bessie asked Sarah.

"Yeh. For ladders."

"And you?" I asked Bessie.

"Naw! She's a cheader! She didn't choose me." Bessie was furious. "That Old Danny Witchie! She looked at me and Sarah and she picked Sarah and left me out!" She rubbed her runny nose on the sleeve of her winter coat. "I hate her like POISON!"

To my amazement, in the gym that morning, Miss Horner had chosen me for the Scottish Quadrille. "I choose only clean, tidy children who know how to stand straight," she snapped. My Bubbie's bones had stood me in good stead.

We were two sets of eight girls of which four in each set were to be "boys". Because I was tall and broadly built, I was to be a boy. Much as I was thrilled to be chosen, I resented having to be a boy.

Caught up in distaste for my imposed role, I grew moody and inattentive, and as we stood in our places ready to begin to rehearse, I heard Miss Horner call my name again and again. "Sophie! Stand up tall! You're a gentleman, you know, a Highland Laddie! In tartan kilt and argyle socks! Up straight now!"

She emphasized the glamour by flicking me lightly with the rubber tip of her long wooden stick.

I felt wronged. I wanted again to be a heroine brought to grace by a noble act. Instead I was to be a boy, a Highland Laddie. In a kilt! What was a Highland Laddie anyway? I wondered. What was a kilt?

By the third lesson, Miss Horner realized I wasn't born to the colours.

"Shame on you!" she raged. "I gave you your Golden Opportunity! I thought you'd be delighted to be a Highland Laddie in the Spring Exhibition -- but I see I was wrong! Go back to your classroom. I'll choose someone else for The Dance! To think I had such Great Expectations for you!"

I was stunned. Such humiliation in front of my peers!

Mamma would be mortified. She had told all the aunties I was to star in the show.

As the days ran by I was in distress. What must I do? How to tell Mamma?

Finally I braced myself.

"Mamma, I'm not in the concert."

"What happened?" Now Mamma was distressed.

"I don't want to be a Highland Laddie."

"What's wrong? What's a Highland Laddie?"

"It's a boy with a skirt ...."

"It's just for fun," Mamma explained. "You like to make fun, don't you?"

"I don't want to be a boy. I want to be -- like in Shule! I want to be like Hannah! That's what I want to be!"

Mamma was silent for a minute.

"Ask the teacher she should give you another chance. Try. It's nice you should be in the school concert."

Luck was with me. One of the girls got the chicken pox and Miss Horner offered me a second Golden Opportunity.

"But remember," she threatened, "I'll be watching you!"

I danced. Now I was a Highland Lassie. The concert was a huge success. Yet there was no joy in it for me.

✿ ✿ ✿

Decades later I was in Scotland for a brief holiday, in beautiful Edinburgh, that historic city of warm people who speak with a musical tongue in a drear climate. This was my first visit, yet the city seemed strangely dear to me. I "did" the shops.

"And will you be attending the Dancing on the Green?" the amiable shopwoman asked as she wrapped my newly purchased cashmere sweater and scarf.

"Oh? Where will this be? I'd love to see the dancing."

"Out there on the great lawn." She pointed to where the rows of bleachers stood bordering the green mown space. I thanked her for her courtesy. "We're very proud of our dancers," she added. "And you have such a fine afternoon to enjoy them."

At two o'clock I joined the other sightseers and dance aficionados on the Green. The mood was high. The tourists were delighted and the Scots responded to their warm appreciation and perpetual picture-taking with civility and complaisance.

I took my seat beside a young woman in a yellow sun-dress with cap to match. As we waited for the performance, we spoke.

"No, I'm not from Scotland. I'm from London," she replied in answer to my question. "Visiting a college friend who was with me at Oxford. She had to pay a hospital visit this afternoon, so I came alone to see the dancing."

I told her I was from Canada and that we grew up singing British songs and learning Scottish dances.

"Do you feel at home in Scotland?" I asked.

"Why, certainly. It's part of Great Britain, isn't it?"

"But are there no historic conflicts in your memory -- tales your grandmother, perhaps, told?"

"Some, I suppose," she tilted her head searching her heritage. "But that was long ago. After all, we are all Britishers, aren't we?"

The entry of three pipers in full regalia piping their martial music interrupted our conversation. They were followed by a group of dancers of various ages, the men in full Highland array, the women in white dresses and slippers. Silver brooches, denoting their clan, pinned their various tartan scarves diagonally to their skirts. As the pipers piped, the company marched around in a circle once or twice, then arranged itself into two parties of eight: four men facing four women. They danced the Quadrille.

How skillfully they performed. How warmly the audience responded to them. Of course the young were nimble and graceful, but I was amazed at the suppleness of the older men, their lightness and their surefootedness. Surely they were born to this dance! All my senses were alive with vicarious pleasure, my nerve-ends taut with alertness.

After several squares, they stopped for a break.

The pipers went into a medley of Men of Harlech, All Through the Night, Skye Boat Song, Annie Laurie. Suddenly, I was weeping, weeping profusely. I didn't even know why I was weeping at this beautiful display on this lovely afternoon.

The young woman beside me was uneasy. "Are you not well?" she asked.

I was not ill. Of course not. I was only struggling, suddenly, with a well of long-repressed tears, tears I hadn't known were there, tears that had congealed in those classrooms of my childhood where the teachers spoke of a Mother Country which was not mine and of which my parents knew nothing. My parents were immigrants, and grateful. But Mother Country? Was Matyushka Russya their Mother Country? And which was mine?

Certainly I had sung those songs of the great deeds of British history that had touched no collective memory in my heart, had been urged to embrace a culture which was strange to my home, to my parents, yet, sure as I lived, it had become my own! Sure as I was sitting on "the Green", I had grown to love those Men of Harlech and Bonnie Prince Charlie of whom our Miss Ransom had so lovingly told us and for whom our little hearts had bled as profusely as did her own hungry romantic heart. And I -- who had found my roots in my parents' remembering (one foot tied to the boat on which I hadn't come, I sometimes thought) -- was it safe for me to love them? Suddenly, I was back in Strathearn School, in Miss Horner's Spring Exhibition where I had been invited to be a Highland Laddie, a role I didn't understand nor want to play, an honour that had no meaning for me.

I wept.

I wept as I had wept for the little Match Girl in the fairy tale who had given her life selling matches on that bitter Christmas Eve. I wept for the Jewish children whose parents had given them no positive sense of themselves as Jews, and for Jews who had beguiled themselves into believing they were Germans, Poles, or Frenchmen, only to become statistics in our ancient history. I wept the unwept tears of the outsider who hungers to belong.

It was some minutes before I could contain myself. My gentle neighbour waited patiently, lovingly rubbing my hand.

"I'm all right now," I said finally. "Thank you for your kindness." I kissed her cheek.

"Would you want to tell me what was wrong?" she smiled at me through her concern.

"I -- I don't quite know ... I -- I think -- I think," I blurted out, "it has something to do with feeling at home ...."

The Joys of Winter

"I hate them! I hate them! I'm not gonna wear them! They itch!" I shouted.

The season had arrived and with it, the long woolen underwear called "vesh", to protect us from the harsh Canadian winter. "And see how my feet look!" I continued to wail. "Like elephants! I can't make my stockings look nice in my boots with the 'vesh' inside!"

"Yeh, and it's hard to go to the toilet -- with the buttons in the back," my little sister Denie added. "It takes so long! Yesterday, I nearly ...."

Mamma was strong on sense. "It's cold outside. Winter you have to dress warm, not fancy."

"I'll better be cold!" I wailed again. "I'm not gonna wear them! Mamma, I'm in Grade Six already. I'm not in baby class! Some of the girls wear brazeers already!"

Mamma was adamant. "In winter you have to dress warm, not fancy."

"So we have high-lace boots and overstockings and rubbers and sweaters and winter coats ...."

"Yeh, and crocheted hats and long scarves and mitts and the little camphor zekela," Denie enumerated, fingering at her neck the cotton camphor bag Mamma had hand sewn for her.

"That's right," Mamma agreed. "That's right. Don't forget the camphor zekela. Comes the winter comes the flu."

Oh, the Canadian winter! The snow banks on Colonial Avenue were so high you couldn't see across to the other side of the street. Horses pulled sleighs down the middle, blazing paths that steamed with hot manure decorated with clusters of sparrows enjoying feast in famine. Snow forts and snowballs abounded. Teams shaped up: boys against girls, one side of the street against the other, this gang against that. Only skating broke down the barriers as we all planned to go to the skating rink at Fletcher's Field to inaugurate the season.

At home, every day brought its crisis. Yesterday it was the "vesh", today it was the skating suit. Papa had made me a pair of knickers, gray English wool with brown check, but I needed a skating sweater.

"Mamma," I pleaded for the ninth time, "Mamma, I need a skating sweater."

"For Chanukah you'll get a skating suit," Mamma announced. A heavy snow had fallen. Chanukah was still a whole week away. Since Tuesday I had been wondering about the great cardboard box in the hall closet.

"Mamma, what's the big box in the hall cupboard?"

Mamma taught patience. "A person had to learn to wait," she replied. "A person has to learn patience. You'll see when it's time ...."

"When, Mamma?"

"Later."

"When later?"

"Chanukah."

So I waited.

The first night of Chanukah fell on Thursday. I rushed into the house after school. The brass Chanukah Menorah was shining on the kitchen table, its two Lions of Judah and the Star of David waiting for the first candle to mark the Feast. The house was fragrant with the freshly rendered chicken fat for Mamma's Chanukah latkes.

"Mamma, everybody's going skating tomorrow night. Can I go?" Mamma granted permission. "Go try on the skating suit."

"Who? Me, Mamma?" I couldn't believe my ears. "What skating suit?"

"It's your Chanukah present. I said for Chanukah .... In the big factory box in the cupboard," Mamma beamed.

"I'll help you," Denie offered as I bounced to take the box. It lay there, almost alive, snuggled in rustling tissue, a mass of bright red fluffy mohair. A large red tam-o'-shanter with bands of red, green and yellow lay on top. There was a sash and a scarf to match. Mamma joined us, glowing with admiration.

"Next year, you, Dinyela. Sophela is older. Her turn first."

For once being older was paying off. Usually it was, "Sophela, you're older. Let her have it this time. She's still a baby."

There was no rancor in Denie. "Take it out," she urged appreciatively, touching it gently. "Put it on. It's soft like a big pussycat."

"It has a funny smell," I ventured as Mamma lifted the massive sweater out of the box and begin to pull it over my head. I sneezed.

"Heptchoo! Heptchoo!" I sneezed in Yiddish.

"Tsum gezunt! Tsum lebn!" Mamma blessed (To your good health! Long life!).

"Heptchoo! Heptchoo!" I sneezed again.

Mamma responded. "You see? You got a cold already! From going without a scarf like I told you."

"No, Mamma! It's from the suit!" I shouted. "Heptchoo! I'm choking! It's from moths!" I struggled to get out of it.

"It's nothing, Sophela. It'll go away. You'll go outside, it'll go away. Till you'll come to the skating rink it won't smell already. Come, look in the big mirror how beautiful you look. A suchy year on me how nice it is!" Mamma was delighted with her purchase.

I held my breath and craned my neck to get as far from the smell as possible as I dashed to the mirror in Mamma's vanity dresser. "Look at me, Mamma!" I pleaded in despair, "I look like a horse! A big red horse!" I burst into tears.

Denie put her arm gently around me. Mamma beamed.

"Twelve dollars and fifty cents I paid for it. Such a bargain. And way? Because it's from moth balls, from last year. In the big stores it costs *twenty-five dollars!* I should live so! That's what the wholesale man said. You should only skate in good health. Go. Go put on the knickers. You'll see how nice!"

"Mamma, I'm melting! Pull it off!" I held my breath, raising my arms to divest myself of the bargain.

Mamma was firm. "Go put on the knickers," she cajoled. "With both together you'll see better."

Papa was a fine tailor and the knickers were beautifully made.

But I was a stocky girl, and while knickers may have been in style, they certainly didn't flatter me.

"See with the knickers?"

Denie was beside me. "With Papa's knickers it's much better," she invoked his beloved image.

"Put on with the sash and tam and scarf," Mamma handed them to me. I obeyed. The broad sash about my middle, the vast tam on my head, I turned to the mirror and doubled up in horror.

"I'm an elephant, a big red striped elephant!" I shouted bitterly. "Now I can't move altogether! If I'll fall down I won't be able to get up! Everyone will laugh at me! I'm not going skating! I'm not!" I dissolved in tears.

Now Mamma was offended. "Shame on you!" she said slowly. "I would want people should laugh from you? Me? Your own mother? That's nice. My enemies shouldn't have such a suit! A beauty! And she's crying yet .... I'm telling you, all the girls will be jealous on you. Some outfit! Like good butter. Try once. You'll see."

✡ ✡ ✡

The moon hung like a silver Chanukah coin in the black sky. The powdered ice, the mounds of snow shimmered beneath the coloured lights over the rink. The skaters were swaying to the rhythms of the Skaters Waltz coming from the changing house. Red sparks flew from its chimney and the scent of burning pine logs hung in the air promising comfort when the cold got too severe.

Me? I sat on the ice, spread-eagled, my new skates glistening in the dark. I couldn't get up. The girls pulled at my arms to lift me. The boys stood around and roared.

"Awright. Now -- everybody together!" Bessie organized. "Pull, everybody, PULL!" I skidded around on my broad bottom but was unable to rise.

"You're pulling out my arms!" I wailed.

Bessie had another idea. "Hey, you guys!" she turned to the boys. "Come on. Help! You go in back and push. Sarah and me'll pull."

But the boys doubled up with laughter. "POOSH!" they cried in chorus. "POOL!"

Bessie begin to feel foolish. "Hey," she scolded me, "ya think we're your servants? Get up yourself!"

I wept with chagrin.

Finally, Hymie the Gorilla was moved to compassion.

"Come on, you guys. Let's give a hand. Sarah and Bessie pull and we'll take her under the arms."

I submitted and after several attempts, I balanced precariously on my skates. "Pull me near the house," I pleaded, "or else I'll fall again." They took my hands and dragged me slowly to the rink's edge. On the snow I managed. I entered the house and changed into my shoes and rubbers.

"That wholesale man cheated your mother," Bessie comforted. "This is a skading suit? It's more a tiboggany!"

"You're right, Bessie. But don't laugh," I tried to regain face. "My father -- my father will buy me a tiboggany. You'll see!" My skating career was at an end.

Tel. PLateau 4653 Res. EAst 9543 **STENZLER BROS.** Dealers in Columbia Phonographs and Records, Radios and Supplies. Full assortment of Musical Instruments. Phonograph Repairs our specialty. Also Sewing Machines Main Office: 748 St. Lawrence Blvd., Montreal.	Compliments of **J. Wiselberg** WHOLESALE AND RETAIL **FURRIER** 1567 St. Lawrence Blvd.
HEFT'S **MEN'S WEAR** HATTERS & HABERDASHERS Two Stores: 3511-4141 ST. LAWRENCE MONTREAL	Tel. LAncaster 6879 **THE BROADWAY MEN'S TAILORING CO.** 3451 St. Lawrence Blvd.
Compliments of **The Fifth Ave. Men's Clothing Co.** 3527 ST. LAWRENCE BLVD. Tel. Lancaster 6988	קאמפלימענטס פון **ר. ווייסבערג** פאריער 3766 St. Lawrence Blvd. טעלעפאן. פלאטא 2520

באזארגט זיך באצייטנס מיט א זאל
אום צו האבן א ליכטיקן. לופטיקן פלאץ פאר חתונות. פארטיס און בעלער
— דאן קומט צו

אנקם האל
קלאסן אין טאנצן
N. H. SINCLAIR. Prop.
142 Fairmount Street West   BElair 3024

מיר דאנקען אלע געשעפטסלייט וואס האבן אנאנסירט אין אונזער זשורנאל

From Yiddishe Kinder, 1927. The Broadway Men's Tailoring Co. belonged to Shulamis' father.

Dora

Dora came into our class mid-term in Grade Six. She had been transferred from another school -- which was odd, since she didn't even live in our district.

I liked Dora. She was a big good-humoured girl with short brown hair, an open face, strong white teeth, and even through her loose jumper one could sense her budding breasts, her broad hips and her stout thighs. Somehow or other, her large shoes always managed to get mixed up with the boys' shoes on gym days.

Dora was two years older than most of us in the class and had been in Canada only three years. We knew she wasn't Jewish; she wasn't English either like the three non-Jewish boys in our class. She was Ukrainian, she said, and I knew what that meant, for Mamma's charwoman, Annie, was Ukrainian, and Mamma spoke Ukrainian to her and gave her our old clothes.

Dora spoke English well enough -- as far as we were concerned -- but whenever she became excited or when she was stumped for an answer, she would explode with Bozsche moy! Ukrainian for My God! For all her lustiness and good humour there was always a strange sad look in Dora's eyes.

I was drawn to her from the start.

Dora was a whiz at arithmetic which made her all the more admirable in my eyes. I invited her to do homework with me at our house after school. She came, we ate our buttered kimmel bread with Mamma's plum jam, drank our milk and sat down to our homework.

Dora admired everything we had, behaved politely and we got through our lessons quickly and happily in time for me to go to Shule afterwards. But she never invited me to her home.

One afternoon, when I entered the classroom, I saw a group of boys in a huddle by the window in the far corner of the room. They were sniggering and Hymie the Gorilla was hoarsely whispering something to them as I took my seat. At first I thought they might be discussing me, but, as Dora showed herself in the door, one boy called out, "Hey, sic it! Here she comes!"

They turned away and Dora took her seat.

I could see she was not happy. She was self-conscious and her teeth were clenched over her lower lip.

"Dora," I whispered, "what's the matter?"

"Nothing," she whispered back without looking up. "Nothing!"

Hymie the Gorilla, who sat beside her, suddenly let out a roar, "Hey, Dora!" and he made an obscene gesture at her with the fingers of both his hands. The class which had turned toward them at his call, was shocked. The boys began to roar; some of the girls giggled into their fists.

I was horrified.

"Shit you! Bozshe Moy!" Dora exclaimed roughly, and put her head on her folded arms on her desk.

Miss Swan, who had been standing in the hall talking to the teacher next door, came in to still the clatter.

"All right, Class. Quiet please!" she called. "What's the matter?"

She was met by dead silence and after a moment, she turned to write some French verbs on the board.

A rustle went through the room. Miss Swan turned to see what was happening.

Noticing Dora's posture, she asked, "What's wrong, Dora?"

Dora didn't answer or lift her head.

"Are you sick, Dora?"

"I'm all right," Dora mumbled through her fists.

"Then sit up and get to work."

When school was out, as soon as we reached the basement Dora left the line and rushed away. I called after her, but she refused to answer. I walked home sadly aware that something cruel was afoot.

Next day, Hymie again made the obscene sign and drew laughter when Dora came into the room. This time, Dora walked up to him, grabbed him by the hair and roared, "Sharrap you! Bozshe Moy! I break your teet! See?" She clenched her large fist at him.

Everyone was too surprised to react. Miss Swan's entrance again brought order to the class. I ached for Dora, but I too was too shocked to say a word.

Right after the Lord's Prayer the following morning, Dora walked into the classroom. Miss Swan was writing on the blackboard. Everything stopped. Dora had her head down and was trying to hide her face from the class. As she tried to ease herself into her seat, Hymie the Gorilla bent over to her and peered into her face.

"Hey! Lookit the shiner!" he shouted. "Who hit ya, Dora? Who hit ya in the lane?"

The boys began to snort. Some of the girls giggled. Dora stood up and ripped out a loud snarl, "Minejerown bizness! Bozshe Moy! Sharrap!"

Miss Swan swung around to face the class. Silence bounced from the walls. I was stunned. Dora's left eye was closed and swollen -- a narrow slit. A terrifying black and blue welt ran all the way down to her puffy upper lip. What we could see of her left arm in her short-sleeved gym blouse was ribboned with frightening black and purple markings.

What could have happened to Dora?

Miss Swan went to Dora's seat.

"What happened, Dora?" she asked softly.

"Notting."

"Yeh?" growled Hymie the Gorilla. "Dat's marks from a ledder strap! Yer fadder hit ya!"

My mouth fell open. I wanted to die. A father hits a child? And with a leather strap? I recalled Papa's comment when his friend Joe broached the subject of physical punishment, "Either you don't need it or it won't help ...."

"He's not my fadder. He's my step-fadder!" Dora hissed through clenched teeth.

"He strapped her good and I know why!" Hymie roared again. A gasp went through the class as everyone trembled lest the secret be revealed.

"Sit down and keep quiet, Hymie!" ordered Miss Swan. "You have work to do. Do it."

But Hymie couldn't stop himself. "Yeh! Yeh!" he continued obscenely. "Dat's why she had to change schools in the middle of the year! Yeh -- with the boys in the lane -- yeh!"

Dora got up, stretched herself to her full height, planted her big feet squarely on the floor and hands on her broad hips, she cried out, "All right, you Hymie Gorilla! All right! Sure my fadder strap me. He got drunk and beat up my Ma and then he strap me because I do f__ with the boys in the lane -- and I don't let him come into my bed! And you, Hymie Gorilla, you mad because I don't do f__

126

wit you! Fah!" She bit her thumb at him. "Fah for you, you no good ...."

The class went into an uproar. I stared at Dora.

There was a strange dignity about her as she defied convention with her terrible confession. I was confused by my mingled reactions of shame for her deed and pride for her strength.

Miss Swan regained her composure.

"Class stand," she ordered. "Everyone line up in two rows outside the room facing right. If I hear one sound, I'll send you all to the office. Dora, go to your seat."

We lined up quickly without a sound. After a few minutes Miss Swan had us return to the room. Dora was not to be seen. "Dora is in the nurse's room. The nurse will look after her well." She stopped for a moment then continued, "I can only feel sorry for Dora, and I think you should all feel sorry for her too. Not all children are as lucky as you are. Now get on with your work. And not another word."

Dora never came back to school. I often wondered what had happened to her.

Reading

Suddenly we were reading.

Friday was Library Day. As the graduating class, Grade Seven, we received library books in school every Friday afternoon. It was the event of the week. Every Friday morning, the teacher would send three boys downstairs to the "Liberry Room". They returned with arms full of books which had been selected for us by the "Liberry Teacher". The books were lined up on the window ledge and we waited in high anticipation for the right to choose.

There was a special ceremony for the book selection. The row that had behaved best during the week, that had most stars on the blackboard, and especially the row that had "sat up" best on Friday afternoon -- hands behind backs, feet flat on floor, head up -- would have first pick. At the teacher's signal, we rose, advanced, took time to make our selection and returned to have our books checked off at her desk.

That year I had chosen to sit at the back of the room by the window. There I could watch the sky and feel the warmth of the large radiators. On Fridays, my attention was riveted on the books, books with well-worn backs, books which generations of Grade Sevens had handled and through which their readers had escaped into distant lands and vicarious experiences.

News of a popular book ran like gossip through the class. "Take The Little Shepherd of Kingdom Come," urged Sarah.

"It's so good! So sad! I cried my eyes out. At the end he dies!"

"Take L.T. Meade," said Bessie. "It's about a poor girl who wants to be a writer. Like you. But she has to work hard for her family because their mother is dead and she has to do all the housework and cook too, and at night she writes and writes nobody should know, and she gets sore hands and the doctor say it's writer's cramp! And her father says it can't be writer's cramp because she never writes. She has to do the housework all day. And the doctor looks at her fingers and he sees the mark where the pencil is always pressing and he asks her. And it's so nice! Because she bursts out crying and tells him her secret that she wants to be a writer! And the father kisses her ...."

Books. Books which led us to the Settlement Library on St. Urbain Street, pushing the perimeter of our lives beyond the school walls; books where not only did girls suffer for their families, but where feelings we harboured in mystery were made manifest.

At that time I acquired a new friend.

Helen was a big girl like me. She lived at another angle from the school and had two sisters who were already working.

Helen and I sat near each other and took our studies seriously. At recess we enjoyed each other's company and gradually set up a pattern of visiting each other on Saturday afternoon.

Often we talked about the books we were reading and Helen told me she read some books her sisters brought home. "Some have lots of love stuff in them," she confided, "but I don't like them too much. I like our hard books better than their True Romance magazines, but sometimes -- I like them ...." she added.

In our house I was enjoying a fling of my own. Mamma had listened to the pleas of a young man who was "working his way through college".

"How could I refuse him, a boy what wants to go to college," she told Papa at lunch one day. "Not Jewish. But very nice. Clean. He wanted I should help him, I should take a pascription for three dollars for a whole year. So I said, 'Send'."

We were already receiving the monthly Yiddish literary magazine, Die Zukunft (The Future), which Papa read and saved from year to year. I hadn't known there were also English magazines until the first issue of The Delineator arrived in the mail.

"For you, Sophela," Mamma had said. "You should read good English."

Mamma and I admired the elegant cover and the slick paper, and I took it to my room. As I turned the glossy pages, I could see nothing that appealed to me.

One picture, however, caught my eye. It was the picture of a stately ship and a young woman standing on the shore looking out to sea. As I turned the page, there she was again, this time in her stateroom, holding a rose as she sat pensively on the edge of her bed.

I was intrigued. The story proved to be the first of a series of monthly adventures of this beautiful young woman who was travelling around the world alone.

But -- *was* she ever alone? Oh no! At every port she met a handsome fellow traveller with whom she became inexorably involved.

Love. This was my first encounter with Love, the forbidden fruit. Did Mamma have any idea of what she had placed before me?

The young lady never married the young-man-of-the-month. There was always some complication. Once she discovered he was a jewel thief hiding from Scotland Yard! Another time he was already married!

I suffered with her each month, and waited impatiently for the weeks to roll by so another issue would arrive. When it appeared, I gulped down my dinner and ran to my room, where, kneeling at the foot of the bed, the magazine spread before me, I embarked on the vicarious adventure that awaited me.

Such excitement!

"Sophie, you'll be late for school!" Mamma would call.

"Soon, Mamma! I'm going ...," and I hurried through the pages I would read again and again at a later time.

One late winter Saturday afternoon, Helen came to visit. Mamma was about to go out. She had been invited to Auntie's for tea, and Denie was going with her.

The house was warm. Before he left for work, Paper had thrown some ashes onto the coals in the furnace to keep it at low comfortable heat.

Mamma liked my friend Helen.

"When you're hungry, take chocolate cupcakes I made -- with milk," she offered.

No sooner were Mamma and Denie out of the house, than Helen exploded. "Look what I brought, Sophie!" She pulled from her purse a Little Blue Book. The title boldly stamped on it was one I had heard whispered in our corner in the school basement but had never thought I'd see.

"It's my sister's," she whispered hoarsely. "It's so dirdy!" I opened my eyes wide.

"It's about a girl. She does such terrible things with men! And such things happen to her! She even has a baby! And -- it's just awful!"

I covered my face with my hands, my mouth soundlessly open, memories of Dora and Winnie flashing through my mind.

"I brought it we should read it together," she continued.

"Here, take it. Look at the first page."

I took the little book in my hands but gave it back quickly. "Helen, we can't read it. If my mother comes in she'll kill me."

"We'll read it fast. It's a small book," she coaxed.

"Come better in the kitchen. My mother left us milk with chocolate cupcakes." I was too excited to look at her.

"Don't you want to read it? Frances, in our class, read it. She says it's scary."

"I'll get the milk from the icebox. In the stove is the chocolate cupcakes."

"Sophie, you're such a baby!" she scolded. "I -- I'm not even hungry yet."

But the tug-of-war in my newly-awakened self was too great for me. "My father -- it's not for me ...."

"So all right. Anyways, I read it already."

As we finished our milk and cake, Helen said, "If I bring it back my sister will know I took it. You want to keep it?"

"No!" I shouted, unable to face the ambivalence of my terrifying desire.

Helen sat down for a moment.

"You know what? Your furnace is going? Let's burn it."

"Burn a book? Helen, what are you saying? Such a terrible thing to do!"

"But you can't keep it. And I can't take it back home."

"So?" I asked quietly, pondering the dilemma.

"So better we should burn it," she hissed.

"So," I acquiesced sadly, "so let's burn it ...."

We opened the furnace door. The fire flared briefly and lay quiescent again.

"You burn the first page," she offered. "It's your furnace."

"No. You." Let her throw the first stone.

Slowly she ripped off the cover and threw it in. A young flame reached up and devoured it.

"Now your turn." She looked me straight in the eye.

With damp fingers I tore out the first page and, with a sigh, threw it into the fire. It too, flared briefly, then turned to ash. Then Helen threw in the next page.

Page by page we destroyed the Little Blue Book, quenching in ourselves the flames that rose up in our young bodies, two child-women in whom the unspoken taboo of our people was suddenly alive.

We stood silently by the open furnace as the last page flickered and turned black, than gray. Then I shut the door.

"I think I'll go home now," said Helen slowly. "Good your mother didn't come in ...." She turned to get her coat. "It was a nice fire, eh Sophie?"

"Yes, Helen. Some fire ...."

"I'll see you in school Monday," she said as she opened the outside door.

Twilight was falling. I went into the dining room and sat down at the oak table, my head on my folded arms. There was a strange silence around me. I had won a Pyrrhic victory. But I knew that Papa and Mamma would approve.

True Romances

It was the custom of Mamma and the aunties to meet on Wednesday afternoons at Bubbie's house. Bubbie served tea and her good yeast dough coffee cake with cinnamon and raisins, or cheese and millet knishes in the downstairs dining room, then they all retired to the upstairs front parlour where Mamma read aloud the week's installments of the Bintel Brief: the letters to the Editor, Forvertz (its "Dear Abby") and the installments of the current novel -- the "roman".

One Wednesday, even before they had had their tea, one auntie said, "Did you hear what happened across the road?"

"Such excitement! Just like in a roman!" said the second auntie.

"When Fate steps in, anything can happen ...," my Bubbie offered.

"I tell you it's hard to believe!" said the first auntie. "The youngest girl, the redhead from across the street, got engaged!"

"You're kidding!" Mamma exclaimed. "When? To whom?"

They were discussing the youngest of the three daughters of the family that lived in the house across the road from Bubbie. She was a pretty auburn-haired young woman whom I had often seen sitting on the step of their large house, reading a book while her two older sisters sat looking into space, hands folded in their laps.

"This week. I heard it by the butcher when I went to buy meat yesterday," explained the first auntie.

"To whom?" Mamma asked again.

"I'm telling you -- it's not to believe. To a nice looking older man with a big moustache and a gold watch and chain across his vest, they say."

"Thank Goodness," said Bubbie. "Such a pity: a decent family with no luck. Such a sad house: three girls and not one of them married. Too bad he didn't want the oldest one. The mother must feel bad: two older girls drying up before her eyes -- not of us be it said -- and the youngest one gets engaged. Just like that ...."

"Each one is born with his own luck," offered Zaida from the rocking chair where he was supposedly reading his paper.

"When a family gets a name for snobs, no one wants to bother with them," countered the second auntie. "No one was good enough for them. Just because they have a piano and their own house ...."

"And they don't have to work in a factory like other people's children -- they think they have to marry a doctor!" added the third auntie.

"Who is he already? Where is he from? What does he do?" Mamma sought particulars.

"They didn't say. They just said he's not from here. He's a big business man but not from here," the first auntie filled in.

Tea was served and the ladies retired to their accustomed place upstairs to catch up on the most recent joys and woes of the world and of their current literary heroine.

But the novel was forgotten in the high excitement of the reality. Why live a paper thrill when there was true romance on their doorstep?

During the next few days I heard Mamma on the phone, questioning her sister-in-law for more news of the engagement, but there was no further information. On Thursday evening following Mamma's afternoon meeting of Peretz Shule Ladies' Auxiliary, I heard her tell Papa, "I tell you, Philip, it's not to believe. It's just like the 'roman'. It should only have a happy ending. They were telling at the meeting what they heard by the butcher in the morning. Everyone was talking about it. Such excitement!" She waited for Papa to lay down his newspaper.

"They say he said he saw her for the first time when he passed on the street before their house on business and she was sitting 'like a flower' (he said) on the steps reading. He fell in love with her right away!"

Papa made a questioning grimace with his eyebrows. "Sounds too good to be true ...."

"He wants to get married right away and take her with him to his big house where he lives ...."

"And nobody knows where he's from?" Papa asked.

"I suppose the family knows, but they didn't say. They wouldn't let a girl go like this .... I'm telling you, it's a miracle."

I was having my lunch next day when I heard Mamma on the phone with Auntie.

"You don't say! You mean it? A ring? A big diamond? From Birks yet? No! Who said? Again by the butcher? Really? Three thousand dollars? I can't believe it! Good. Come here for tea."

In the evening, Mamma again reported to Papa. "You see? You can never tell when good luck will strike. Imagine! A Three Thousand Dollar Diamond Ring from Birks he gave her! He must be very rich. A rich business man. He paid with a cheque and he wants the wedding should be Saturday night just the family, and they should leave right away Sunday morning because he has to get back to his business."

"Where is his business? Where is he taking her to?" Papa pressed again.

Mamma only knew what Auntie had learned at the butcher's that morning.

If the affair was exciting to Mamma, to me it was pure magic. All my fairy tales about princes coming from far-off lands to woo the beautiful sad stepchild suddenly came to proof. Here it was right before my eyes -- a lovely young girl living in such a sad dejected household and suddenly, a prince -- nay, a King, since he's much older -- comes from a far-off land and finds her on her own doorstep, and wants to marry her right away and take her on a far-off journey to his far-off castle! A thrilling tale. There was even an aura of mystery about it!

When the family assembled as usual at Bubbie's house on Saturday night, there was a pall over the room.

"A pity! Such a pity!" mourned my Bubbie who had learned the culmination of the story in the women's balcony in the synagogue that morning.

"How does the proverb go?" said my Zaida. " 'It seems to me my neighbours are laughing, but they're really sobbing' ...."

"You think the sun is coming out, but instead, lightning strikes you," said the first auntie.

"A shock," said Zaida gain. "But thank Heaven it turned out like this. It's Gam zu l'tovah (all for the best). When you think what could have happened!"

"Sometimes it does happen," said the youngest auntie, the unmarried one, with a sad look in her eye. "Sometimes a rich man does come from another city and wants to marry a poor girl ...."

"I kept asking where he's from," said Papa. "I read in the papers about these men who come from South America and capture white young girls for their 'houses'." (He used the Yiddish diminutive which implied a special kind of 'house'.)

There was a prolonged silence.

"How did they find out?" asked Mamma.

"The cheque he gave to Birks. It was no good. There's no such account in the bank in South America like he gave them."

"You can't fool around with a store like Birks," said an uncle. "They have their ways to find out fast."

"But what does he say?" asked Mamma.

"Say? He doesn't say. He just disappeared. He said he was going downtown to fix it all up with them -- and he never came back...."

"Imagine! Imagine!"

There was dead silence in the room, broken only by the second auntie who suddenly said, "At least she had one moment of joy in her life. What did the other sisters have? Nothing!"

"With daughters you have to be so careful," mused Mamma.

" 'Small children don't let you sleep; big ones don't let you live'," quoted Zaida again.

Everyone sipped tea in silence. Each was wrapped in his or her own fears, in his or her own fantasies.

"America!" said an uncle.

"Such times we're living in," mourned Mamma. "Whoever heard of such things in Chernobyl?"

For me, this sudden denouement was unbelievable. How could a fairy tale have such an unhappy ending?

My First Party

Towards the end of Grade Seven, our final year at Strathearn School, the girls of our class were invited by Miss Ethel Shayne of the newly inaugurated Neighbourhood House to form a club. The Neighbourhood House was a community project of the National Council of Jewish Women -- a project established to keep the young off the streets and to integrate them happily into the community.

How special we felt! How grown up! Grade Seven, the Graduating Class! We had also begun to feel our sexual differences and there were signs of puppy love in the air.

That boy in the second seat first row was a nice boy. He was older and taller than the rest of us, a gentle, soft-spoken lad who loved to draw.

I was full of admiration.

"When he draws a tree it really looks like a tree," I told Mamma. And to him I said, "How can you make it so real?"

"And you?" he responded gallantly, smiling, but not looking up at me, "You write such good compositions. And Poetry yet!"

When he showed me the drawing of an old sea captain he had copied from a tin of Old Salt Sardines, I was overawed.

"It's so real! His eyes like a real old man! And his beard ... and his mouth with the pipe!"

Even our teacher was impressed. "Benjamin has a special gift," she said. I was very happy about Benjamin.

In our corner of the girls' basement, Miss Shayne's offer was very warmly discussed at recess and at lunch time. Finally we decided to accept. The name Miss Shayne suggested for our club was the Merry Sorority. None of us knew what a sorority was, but Merry we liked, like in Merry Xmas. A girl named Frances, who had older sisters who knew about such things, said they liked the name. "It's like in College, they say," she reported to us. "With a nice name you could have parties and invite nice boys."

The Neighbourhood House on Laval Avenue was a pleasant place with airy rooms and banners of flowered draperies at the large windows. Miss Shayne welcomed us warmly and told us we would meet every Thursday at four o'clock. She also told us we would elect an "executive" and keep "minutes". She explained the terms briefly and added, "You will pay five cents at each meeting and the Treasurer will buy a book in which the Secretary will write your Minutes. The rest of the money will be for refreshments when you have a party."

Our elections were by acclamation and were based on logic. Because Frances had those knowledgeable sisters, she was elected President. Bessie was best in Arithmetic, so she was chosen Treasurer. I, Sophie, was elected Secretary because I was "so good in composition and poetry".

On the way home from the meeting, we all accompanied Bessie to Malo's where, armed with the first collection of five cent pieces, we bought a special exercise book for Minutes. I accepted the book with pride, well aware of my responsibility, and spent that whole evening after Shule fashioning the Minutes of our first meeting according to Miss Shayne.

As time went on, I discovered that the lyrics remained pretty much the same. Only the melody changed.

> Week 1: The girls of the Merry Sorority Club had their first meeting at the Neighbourhood House. Miss Shayne said we should elect an Executive. Frances is President, Bessie Treasurer and Sophie is Secretary. We have to pay 5 cents a week for refreshments for parties. Frances said we should have a party right away. We will talk about it again next week.
>
> The meeting was adjourned.
>
> Week 2: The girls of the Merry Sorority had their second meeting at the Neighbourhood House. Sophie read the Minutes of the first meeting. Frances said we should have a party. With boys. We have to have a house for the party. A few girls said they'll ask their mothers.
>
> The meeting was adjourned.
>
> Week 3: The girls of the Merry Sorority had their third meeting at the Neighbourhood House. Sophie read the Minutes of the second meeting. Frances asked which girl could give her

house for the party. Nobody's mother said yes. We will speak about it again next week.

The meeting was adjourned.

Week 4: The girls of the Merry Sorority had their fourth meeting at the Neighbourhood House. Sophie read the Minutes. Frances said her mother said she could have the party in their house. Her mother will bake a big cake, and we could buy the ginger ale from the club money. Frances' big sisters said they will help with the program. The party will be in two weeks, Friday night at 7 o'clock. With boys!

The meeting was adjourned.

Week 5: The girls of the Merry Sorority had their fifth meeting at the Neighbourhood House. Sophie read the Minutes. Everyone was glad the party will be next week. Some of the girls said we should have some boys from the class and some from the other Grade Seven. But Frances said Grade Seven boys are too babyish. She said we should invite some bigger boys -- girls' brothers. But some of the girls don't want their brothers at the party and they don't know other boys to ask. So everybody said, "So let be with the boys from the class." We decided we won't have a meeting next week because it's before the party.

The meeting was adjourned.

I had kept Mamma au courant about the Merry Sorority party. "Ma, they'll come," I reported finally, "the boys from the class."

"That's nice," said Mamma. "So for your first party you need a new dress."

I was thrilled. Except when I heard that Benjamin could not come. He worked in the drugstore late Friday night. My heart sank. All the boys would be there, but not Benjamin! I dared not say a word.

Mamma kept her word and bought me a new dress for the party. It was peach coloured, of a silky stuff -- a square dress with a short accordion-pleated skirt and a big rose hand painted on the bodice.

Mamma was very proud of her purchase. "It's the new style -- a flapper dress," she announced. "Good that we have a friend with a factory. Only two left, he told me. Put in on."

This was my first "brought" dress. Until then, my auntie had cut out dresses for me and Mamma had sewn them on her Singer treadle sewing machine in the dining room. Sometimes she even embroidered them with a butterfly.

"A grown-up dress," Mamma emphasized. "The rose is hand painted. In gold yet."

Like Cinderella's sisters I pushed and pulled. I finally squeezed myself into the dress, but it clung to my budding breasts and reached halfway up my pubescent thighs.

"Mamma, give it back," I pleaded. "It's not for me."

"It's the style," she said. "Flapper dresses is very short."

"But look how tight it is for me!"

"I can't give it back," Mamma acknowledged. "He told me they don't take back in a factory. He says he took one for his girl too -- Essie, you know. Same age like you."

But age had little to do with it. Mamma's friend's daughter was a slight sophisticated little girl who already used face powder from a "compact". She had shown it to me when we had visited. I was a Borodensky whose daughters were tall broad-hipped buxom women and at twelve I was already showing signs of following the family design.

"I can't wear this dress!" I pleaded. "Look how short it is! My pulkess are sticking out! The boys will see everything."

But it was no use. I wore the flapper dress and stood in a corner all evening, hiding behind one girl or another, comforting myself with the knowledge that at least Benjamin was not there.

The party was not a total success. No matter how hard Frances' sisters tried, they couldn't get us to mingle. I need not have worried about my dress. I was properly hidden by the girls who clustered against one wall while the boys clustered against the other. There was whispering from the girls' side and sniggering from the boys'.

Refreshments finally broke the ice. Frances' mother had prepared a lovely big cake with pink icing and we had brought the ginger ale. The table also boasted two dishes of raisins and almonds and a large bowl of fresh fruit.

At first all went well. Everybody was busy eating and drinking. Then the boys became a bit raucous. A fat boy named Issie grabbed a banana and waving it at his friends, mumbled something. The boys began to laugh and to scramble for the rest of the bananas, boisterously comparing them for size amid guffaws of laughter. And we knew what that meant! One boy even dared explode the word "brazeer"!

We were mortified.

Frances' big sisters could not be seen. We could hear their stifled guffaws from the kitchen.

When we met on the next Thursday for our meeting of the Merry Sorority, nobody mentioned the party. My minutes read:

> Week 6: The girls of the Merry Sorority had their sixth meeting at the Neighbourhood House. Sophie read the Minutes of the fifth meeting. Because is it nearly end of school, we decided this was the last meeting.
>
> The meeting was adjourned.

The Four Doors

Mamma always dreamed of having her own house.

"At home in Chernobyl we always lived in our own house," she often said. "Chassia Dobkin's house was well known in Chernobyl. My father, Shloime, I don't even remember. I was three years old when he died that Purim day. I recall the loud wailing that suddenly arose. Then someone put a moon cookie into my hand and took me away. Where? I can't remember. But we always lived in our own house."

Papa had heard all this before. "Why do we need a house?" he asked again. "A house needs a man who is handy with tools and can look after it. Me? I'm in the tailor shop from early till late. It's not for me."

"But Philip ...."

"Vichna, Stop it. A man in business needs his money for his business."

"But a woman needs a house," Mamma insisted. "When all the sons were gone," Mamma referred to her brothers, "and I left for America, my mother sold the house with an agreement that as long as she lived she could have a room there under her own roof. She lived till eighty seven and the people looked after her till she died. 'Chassia the Wise' they called her -- not for nothing."

"America is different." Papa was impatient. "And anyway, I'm not good for a landlord."

Nevertheless, on the following Sunday morning, I answered the doorbell to admit Mr. Katz, the buttonhole maker who worked for Papa after his day at the factory.

I was a little afraid of Mr. Katz with his rolling Russian country speech unfamiliar to the Yiddish of my environment, but I liked looking at him. He was a tall handsome man who had seen military service in Russia. He wore a gray karakul Cossack hat on his thick black hair and his broad shoulders were square in the greatcoat Papa had tailored for him. His manner was genial but businesslike, the manner of the perfect go-between. I had heard Mamma say he bought and sold houses on the side.

"And from every deal he licks a good fat bone," she added, a touch of envy mixed with her admiration.

Mr. Katz owned three flats on St. Urbain Street near Duluth. He spoke proudly of them as his "three doors". "My three doors," he assured us, "palaces! I live in the downstess and I rent out the two upstesses. (His use of the 'Royal I' included his family.) "Rooms? I tell you -- you could make a wedding in each room! Specially the double-polla -- like a big field! And I have a fine yard. Eight chickens and a rooster already. And two geese. And eggs? Every day for breakfast I eat my own two fresh eggs! And geese? Fatter every day! We'll have some goose-fat for the Festivals!"

"Just like God in Odessa!" Mamma conjured up the ultimate image of bliss. "Nu, Philip?" She gave Papa a meaningful look.

"I spoke to Mr. Philip a few times already he should buy a house. I could get him a real bargain, but you know his answer ...," said Mr. Katz. Then, turning to Papa, "Today, Mr. Philip, I came to invite you we should go in business together. There is four doors on Maple Street -- four doors -- I tell you, beauties. Such a year on me! Bright. Sunny. And we could get it for a song. Rented. All rented. With good tenners. Fourteen and eighteen dollars a month -- four and five rooms. I'm telling you -- a find! A regular milch cow! Mr. Philip, come see for yourself!"

Mamma had mixed feelings. "Mr. Katz, I want a house we should live in it ourself. Not rent out. And over there is not a good neighbourhood for growing girls."

"So? You'll take the rent from there and you'll live somewhere else," Mr. Katz solved the problem. "No trouble." He looked at Papa who stood in contemplation by the window.

"Mr. Philip, what do you say? I'll make an appointment we should go see it together."

There was the thrill of ownership in the air. Mamma seemed ready to compromise. She liked successful men like Mr. Katz. Her red head tilted to one side, she said, "Nu, Philip?"

Papa was ill at ease. "I should be a landlord?" He shrugged it off. "It's not for me."

Nonetheless, next Sunday morning he and Mr. Katz went to see "the doors", and before long, we were greeted with the news that a decision had been reached -- to buy.

"Bright rooms ... big rooms," Papa agreed. "And nice people. Upstairs -- a beautiful little boy, Samela!"

"I told you it's good!" Mr. Katz was triumphant. "You'll see -- from this house we'll buy another and another yet. You just leave it to Morris Katz!"

Mamma feared a mixed blessing. She was quite willing to get rich but was afraid of losing Papa's money. "Let's hope you're right, Mr. Katz," she said. "Still I wish we should have better a house we could live in ourself ...."

"One thing," Papa said suddenly. "No baths. The doors have no baths. How can you let people live without baths?"

"What do you care?" Mr. Katz was a realist. "They're happy? Leave them!"

"We'll have to put in baths," Papa insisted.

On the first Sunday of each month Papa and Mr. Katz visited "the doors" to collect the rent. As the money rolled in in the first three months, Mr. Katz exulted, "Nu, Mrs. Philip? Like I told you -- a regeler milch cow!"

In the fourth month, at Papa's insistence, bathtubs were installed. "You can't let people live like pigs," he argued. While Mr. Katz suggested that tin tubs were good enough, Papa insisted, "If you're buying, you buy the best. After all, I'm buying for my own house!"

The bill which they paid within ten days -- from their own pockets to obtain the whole discount -- come to three months rent.

While Mamma never mixed into business affairs, she considered "the doors" common property. One Sunday, when Papa came home, I heard Mamma ask, "They paid?"

"They paid."

"They like the baths?"

"Sure they like. Why not? The best white deep baths. Like I would like for myself ...."

"That's nice."

For a while Papa was absorbed in his newspaper. Then he said, "But now ...," he hesitated with the news, "now Samela's mother says she wants a new sink. She says this one is old and gets rusty and she has to work hard to get it nice."

"My black dreams on her head!" Mama exploded. "Such chutzpah! She always had it like this! So? A house gets old just like a person."

"She showed me. It's true," Papa spoke quietly. "It does get rusty." He paused. "A nice bright kitchen with embroidered cross-stitch curtains she made herself -- and the sink looks bad."

"So?" Mamma was defiant.

"I'm afraid we'll have to put in sinks. It's our propity after all."

"But we don't even live there!"

"Even if we sell it, it's good. We'll get back our money."

"Philip, you're not asking me, but I'm telling you -- I'm against it!" Mamma was practically in tears. "Times are getting worse. Don't put in any more money!"

Papa closed the door on the discussion. "Vichna, don't mix into business. Leave it to the men!"

The "four doors" get new sinks.

"They like the sinks?" Mamma asked resentfully.

"Nice stainless steel sinks. Why shouldn't they like? They won't get rusty."

"Stainless steel yet?" Mamma's voice rose. "What's wrong with white?"

"For a few dollars more you get the best." This was Papa's Principle. "It's good and it lasts longer."

"They should live so long like a white sink lasts meanwhile!" Mamma was furious. "For me and my family is good enough a white kitchen sink and washtub, and for our tenners only stainless steel? Ai, Philip!"

"I'm telling you again, Vichna, Don't mix in! You don't know business!"

The argument was settled. Mamma turned away and Papa again turned to the coloured picture supplement of the Sunday Forward.

As the months wore on, Samela's father began to work only part time, then eventually lost his job. The other tenant husbands were also laid off -- at first temporarily, then permanently. The Depression was on.

The rent remained unpaid first one month, then another. Soon two of the tenants were five and six months behind. The money for the sinks and tubs had not yet been recouped.

One Sunday, when Papa and Mr. Katz returned from "the doors" their faces showed strain.

"Philip, what happened?" Mamma was alarmed.

"One downstess burned the door from the kitchen in the stove. They have no coal."

"We'll send them a loyess letter," Mr. Katz's voice was harsh. "We'll make them move!"

"In the middle of winter? So? Where will they go? With young children yet!" Papa's anguish was clear.

"It's not our business! We got to pay taxes!"

"We'll wait another month. Maybe it'll get better. Maybe it'll change."

Mama wrung her hands, staring at Papa.

"Vichna, don't say a word! I told you I'm not good for a landlord! For me it's not tenners -- it's people!"

Taxes were pressing, and Mr. Katz finally decided it was no use sending good money after bad. "Let it go for taxes," he said mournfully one Sunday morning after much talk. "What can you do? It's bad everywhere."

"And your own doors?" Mamma asked, indirectly striking out at Papa.

"My own doors I'll keep. I paid the taxes."

"You and your milch cow!" Mamma could not contain her pain. Eyes brimming, she left the room.

Papa and Mr. Katz looked at each other in silence. Finally, Mr. Katz spoke. "Women!" he exploded. "What do they know of business!"

"What can you do?" said Papa stoically.

"What do they know!" Mr. Katz repeated as he let himself out the door.

Transitions

The fairy tale years were at an end and soon we were in the Real World of High School where our teachers repeatedly informed us that we weren't babies anymore, and that the next four years would determine where we would find our place in the outside world.

Papa and Mama agreed that I would attend Baron Byng High School which was famous for a high level of achievement in the Academic Course it offered which included Latin, Music and Art. This course prepared students for university entrance, in comparison with Commercial High which led to the business world.

Actually, Mamma had given in to Papa.

"How much learning does a girl need till she gets married?" she said. However, as the years progressed, it was Mamma who encouraged me to study.

Once again I was in a Protestant school where 99.9% of the population was Jewish. Here, however, there was not a single Jewish teacher on staff. Even holding a B.A. degree, few Jewish teachers were hired and those who were could only teach in the Elementary School. They were placed in Grades Four to Six, which meant they had a $50.00 per annum advantage over teachers with a one year Intermediate Diploma from Macdonald College.

The year went pleasantly by. My literary bent, which had been inculcated at home and strengthened in the Peretz Shule, flourished, even as I limped along in mathematics.

"Instead of algebra, her math notebook is filled with her poetry," Mamma reported to Papa on her meeting with my teacher. But the world opened up before me. Girlfriends, boyfriends appeared, then changed as we tried out our different tastes in search of our own persona. I had a special problem: I needed friends who also shared my Jewish interests in the writers and scholars who came to visit, and in the Yiddish Theatre which was then at its height in Montreal, and there were few such in my class. I also dreamed of going to Columbia University in New York to study journalism.

The Wall Street crash of '29 put an end to that dream. The white blouse, navy tunic and black stockings leveled our economic situation in the high school classroom, but the fees at any university spelled out the difference. Most girls would end up as office help or salespeople in small shops. The few whose parents could afford it, would go to teachers' college in the hope of being placed with the Protestant School Board.

September. We had just returned to the city after the traditional summer in the country. Much of that time had proved a nightmare for me as I went to the post office each evening waiting for the envelope which would bring the matriculation results. In mid-August it arrived; I had even passed my math exams and had a sufficient aggregate mark to enter McGill University. Yet autumn, which usually found me busy, found me at loose ends.
"So what do you want to be?" Mamma asked again.
"You know what I want -- but it can't be!" I exploded.
"My daughter has to be different ...," Mamma responded. "Maybe you should go to Business College, like the other girls, after all!"
I bolted. "Mamma, it's not for me. I don't want to work in an office!"
"You're not thinking of what the Principal said you should be!" She looked at me in horror.
Mamma was referring to the day our High School principal had visited our class just before matriculation exams.
"Soon you will be leaving us to go your separate ways," he said. "What are your plans? Perhaps some of you do not even realize what you are suited for." He paused. "We who have observed you all these several years, know your potential better than most people. Yet, which of you will come to ask our opinion or advice?"
I went.
First he congratulate me. "I hear you've been chosen valedictorian." I acknowledged the honour.
"I came to ask what you would advise me to do after I leave high school," I began. I was expecting the beginning of a dialogue about the Literary Life since I was known to be writing poetry and did so well in literature.
To my astonishment, he said, "You are so good at dramatics. Why don't you become an actress?"
He had touched a nerve.

How did he know my repressed childhood fantasy, the dream which awoke in me when I saw my first play, Joseph and his Brethren, at the graduation of the Jewish Peretz Shule? I flashed back to my tenth year when, fancying myself a great actress, I had slipped down those icy stairs on Colonial Avenue. And then to my reputation as "star" at the Shule since the time I had, in one weekend, memorized all ninety-two stanzas of Frug's The Sexton's Daughter to compete for the honour of reciting it at the Chanukah concert -- and had won! Did he know about that? There had been little opportunity at Baron Byng to show myself in that light.

It was different with literature in which everyone knew I shone. I had replaced the first dream with that of being a writer.

The memory of the book I had begun to write when I was ten flashed by. I recalled how I had dropped dear Beth Belmont of the Storms when I discovered I was putting her through the trials of Little Women. I still had that shiny blue exercise book with its first twenty-two pages covered in blue copybook writing.

I thanked him quickly and rushed from the room.

I can still hear Mamma when I told her.

"An actress?! My daughter should be an actress?! A fine thing! He's crazy! That's a life for a young Jewish girl?"

"I know, Ma. I knew you'd say that ...."

"What else should I say?" She looked at me in consternation. "It's nice to go to the theatre sometimes. I like a good drama myself. But, my own daughter should go on the stage?" Her voice trembled. "Such a life they have! Na-v'nad! Now one place, now another. And family life? What kind of family life do they have? Whose wife is whose husband's? Feh! It's not for us." She paused again. "People like us don't become actors."

"You know I always wanted to be a writer," I offered my alternative choice knowing I was stepping on tenuous terrain. "I always wanted to go to Columbia University ...."

"All those writers you met through the Shule!" she interrupted me. "The Shule put such ideas in your head. My daughter has to be different!" We were quiet for a minute.

"I know," she continued sadly. "I know you always wanted to go to Columbia and learn to be a writer, but who has so much money? Such a Depression! Better think of something else." Speaking to no one in particular, she returned to the principal's suggestion. "An

actress he thinks she should be. With her poems and everything ....
If that's his best idea, better he should keep quiet."

She left the room.

One Friday evening, when I was visiting my classmate, Anne, she said, "I'm going to Macdonald College to become a teacher."

"A teacher?"

Macdonald College of McGill University housed three schools on its beautiful campus in Ste. Anne de Bellevue: the schools for elementary school teachers, for agriculture and for homemakers. It had started out as a school for farmers, then had branched out to include their children and their wives. Its insignia was a gold triangle on a green field. Tuition was free, but one had to pay thirty-two dollars a month (eight dollars a week) for board and lodging.

"Anne," I said wistfully, "you know there are no jobs, especially for Jewish girls. Don't you remember what happened last year when we went to apply for training as kindergarten teachers in answer to the School Board's letter? 'Girls of the Hebrew persuasion cannot be expected to teach the Christmas story with conviction,' the Supervisor said, and she sent us away, even though the Board was asking for girls to apply!"

"I know, I know," Anne replied sadly. "But I'm going anyway. My parents want me to go and I want to go. Maybe things'll change. Look, what else can I do?" She was suddenly angry.

"Maybe I'll go too," I ventured. "I used to make concerts with the kids in the country every summer."

"You'll be good at it," she replied without looking at me.

This time Mamma was pleased "That's nice. To be a teacher is nice. I'll ask Papa. You think they'll take you?"

"I'll try ...."

Papa too, was pleased. There was only the matter of the three hundred and twenty dollars for board and lodging.

Then the miracle happened. The factory above Papa's shop suffered a fire. "The sprinklers on my ceiling wet the stock. All the English wools," he mourned.

Mamma contained herself as best she could. "So what will you do?"

"I called the insurance. They know it's not my fault. I'll see what they'll say," Papa was his usual stoical self. I held my breath in quiet prayer.

On the following Monday, when Mamma answered the phone, I heard her say, "Nu, thank God, Philip. Now you'll be able to buy new materials."

When Papa came home, he said to me, "Send away the application to the College."

"But the money, Papa ...."

"We'll use the insurance money. They'll give me three hundred and fifty dollars." He smiled. "Just enough for living there and thirty dollars left for the year spending money."

"But Papa, the money is for material! You have to buy material for your work!"

"Meanwhile I sent it all out to dry. Anyway, the wholesaler said my name is good. They'll sell me what I need."

The tale ends happily. Papa's material dried out without damage. I was accepted into Macdonald College, and was off on the high seas toward the career to which I would devote most of my life.

Kasha and Loving Kindness

Papa was a great believer in moderation.

"It's the 'too' that's no good," Papa said, looking to the rocking chair where I sat reading a book. "Too good is as bad as too bad; too clean as bad as too dirty; and too much as too little."

I listened.

" 'Spare the rod and spoil the child!' " quoted Papa's friend Joe who admired Papa and always threatened to run away with Mamma. Papa was his mentor.

"Well ...." Papa had reservations about the rod. "I always say a rod doesn't help. About the *too*, I know that too much is sometimes worse than too little. When I was a child I liked beans. But when the tailor to whom I was apprenticed fed me beans twice a day for two years ...."

"So that's why you don't eat beans!" I ventured.

"I can't stand cold potatoes," offered Joe, "or tinned fish. As a boy in Russia, during the war, all we could get was frozen potatoes and tinned fish. Those hunger years -- they're still in my belly ...."

My own trial by excess occurred when I was preparing to leave for Macdonald College.

My Bubbie was very proud that I, her eldest grandchild was to be a teacher. Like most women of her generation, she had had very little education. A Jewish girl's education was usually limited to the reading of the Tseena Urena, a book of prayers in Yiddish especially designed for women, prayers connecting Jewish values through biblical heroes and heroines to their own daily needs.

Like so many Jewish mothers she revered learning. Her own children had gone to work early in the Golden Land to help support the family. That I, her first grandchild, should go to college and become a teacher was a great gift God had bestowed upon her. When she heard the news, she asked me to come to lunch.

"I'll make you something special," she said. "A maichol," she added the Yiddish word for a treat. "Something I know you like."

I loved Bubbie's cooking and that she was showing her love and approval in this way was very gratifying to me.

When I arrived, she said, "Tochterl, I know you like kasha (buckwheat), so I made some nice chicken soup with kasha."

"Wonderful, Bubbie." It was one of my favourite dishes.

In my Bubbie's house there were no middle-sized portions. When Bubbie brought you a plate of soup it was filled to the edge of its broad flat rim. If you ate it all, she would invariably say, "Would you like a little more, dear?" If you didn't finish, she would say, "What's wrong? Don't you like it or aren't you feeling well?"

The soup was delicious, rich and golden with glowing coins of chicken fat floating on it, guarding like a treasure, the plump fluffy kasha on the floor of the white plate. I ate every bit of it, and so, of course, Bubbie said, "How about a little more, Tochterl?"

Knowing this was just the beginning. I said, "What else have you got, Bubbie?"

She tightened the traditional white kerchief she wore.

"I know you like kasha," she said, a modest smile on her pale lips, "so I made a roast with kasha." And turning to the big black coalstove, she picked up the plate she had prepared and placed it before me, steaming and savoury, filled as before to the very edge.

The beautiful kasha was swathed in rich delicious natural gravy, and enthroned upon it sat large chunks of succulent beef, fragrant with onion and bay leaf and a hint of garlic. My nostrils quivered as I settled in to enjoy the delicacy, in no way even conscious of my usual concern with gaining weight. All I knew was that it was superb, that my Bubbie was, as always, the best cook in the world, and that it was as much a joy for her to sit and watch me put away that food as it was for me to be eating it.

By this time, my hunger had receded. As my tempo slowed down, showing that I might not be able to finish all the dish held, my Bubbie was concerned. Inevitably came the question:

"What's the matter dear? Don't you like it, or aren't you feeling well?"

"It's delicious, Bubbie," I replied contentedly, "but I'm really quite full. You gave me so much ...."

"I don't know what's happening to the young people today," she mused. "In my time a meal was a meal. Now -- a thimbleful -- and they're full!"

I laughed and sat back languorously to talk with her, when she got up again, her hands clasped under her large white apron.

"Tochterl, I made you something special for desert. I made some knishes -- potato knishes with kasha -- for dessert."

My Bubbie's knishes with kasha were famous among all who knew her. She had taken the trouble to make them especially for my lunch. Empty or full to bursting, how could I refuse?

I sat in front of the flaky, delicately-browned pastry, wishing I had not eaten any of the soup or quite so much of the main dish. Although I dreaded disappointing her, it was no use. I was just too full of kasha to do more than take just one bite. I could see it coming.

"What's the matter, dear? Don't you like it or ...."

"Bubbie, darling," I gasped, "nobody cooks as well as you do. It's just delicious. But I can't eat another bite."

"A pity," she said. "Such good knishes. Nu, I'll tell you what: If you can't eat them now, I'll wrap them in wax paper and you can take them with you. You'll have them for supper."

I thanked my Bubbie for her goodness and kissing her lovingly, wondering when I would again ever be able to eat kasha. Strangely enough, when Mamma placed the reheated knishes on the table that evening, mine was the first hand to reach out to the plate!

Leaving Home

I don't recall the last days before leaving for Macdonald College. I don't recall where I bought those antiseptic looking white and blue striped uniforms with the separate white starched collars we wore that year, or even when I sewed all those name tapes on them and on my other linens. Surely Mamma must have helped. I can't even recall clearly that last evening when I must have been busy sorting and packing, with my beloved Denie proudly assisting me in the living room as I layered my possessions into my newly purchased valise.

True, there had been high excitement, with Mamma on the phone telling everyone the great news that her Sophela was "going to collitch, the first in this family ...."

Where was Mamma that last evening? Surely she was there, at home, yet I can't place her presence in our midst.

The morning of my leaving is very vivid in my mind. Mamma, who rarely got up for breakfast with us, appeared outside my bedroom, fully dressed.

"Come eat. It's ready," she announced.

I was too excited to eat.

"Just coffee," I said as I sat down at the table.

"Take toast," Mamma offered in a strained voice, "and a medium egg like you like it."

"I'm not hungry, and we have to leave soon. Why isn't Papa here yet? He said he'll take me to the train."

"If he said, he'll be," Mamma's voice quivered. "He just went to open the store. He'll be here. Eat. Sit with me a minute."

We sat in silence, Mamma's eyes glued to the white enamel tabletop, my untouched breakfast growing cold before me.

"You want to tell me something, Mamma?"

"What should I tell you?" She didn't raise her eyes. "I'll ask you a question better." She paused again as though she were seeking the answer to the Riddle of Happiness for me.

In our bedroom, Denie was preparing for school, lingering longer than was her wont.

"What is it, Mamma?"

Which important question does a mother ask her daughter just before she leaves her home for the first time? I wondered.

"You're glad you're going?"

"Sure I'm glad."

"Tell me. Do you ...." She paused again, then looked straight into my eyes. "Do you smoke?" she asked as though everything depended upon my answer.

I was puzzled. *This* was her question?

"I don't," I answered truthfully.

"Your friends, do they smoke?"

"Yes, they do."

"You're sure you don't?"

"I don't." Then suddenly, "But if I'll want to, I will!"

Mamma burst into tears.

What was all this about? I wondered. I had tried smoking when my friends did, but didn't like it. I knew I had other things I wanted to do with my money. So why was she making such a fuss over it?

"Why are you crying, Mamma?"

"I'm crying ...," but she couldn't finish her sentence for sobbing.

Suddenly I felt powerful. I was seventeen and I was leaving home. I must be independent. Mamma mustn't make me feel like a baby! "I'm leaving home and I'm going to be a teacher! I'm leaving home!" a two-part voice chorused within me. I jumped up to wipe out the quavering one.

"Mamma! If I'll want to, I'll smoke!" I returned to my room in disproportionate anger.

Such nonsense! I don't even like it! I thought, but I refused to say anything more aloud.

When Papa arrived to take me to the station, Mamma was still crying. Denie, who had not shown herself all morning, came into the room with her coat on, her books in her arm. She kissed my cheek and with a quick, "Bye, Soph!" she slammed the street door behind her.

Papa looked at Mamma, then picked up the valise.

"We'll go now," he said.

When I arrived at Macdonald College and opened my luggage, I found a note from Denie. It read,

Dear Soph,
Please don't be angry with Mamma.
She really loves you.
Good luck.
                    Love,
                        Denie

I was stunned. Denie had understood.
And I? I was too busy being "grown up" to see ....
And Mamma? Mamma crying? Mamma could no longer call me back -- to tighten a bow or to pin a hanky onto my dress ....

I Become a Teacher

Macdonald College! I revelled in its vast campus, its fine salmon-coloured brick buildings, its huge tapestry-like willows in which I sat to study or to write a poem. I loved my classes and was enthralled by the adult approach of my professors as they opened new worlds to me. The practice-teaching sessions in Montreal brought both fear and delight as well as a vision of tomorrow. I participated in the extra-curricular activities offered by the Student Council and even had a boyfriend who escorted me to College dances.

Life was exciting, yet I was constantly worried; over and over again, the Dean warned that there were few jobs in Montreal awaiting the 167 students, and that meant even fewer jobs would be available to the 44 Jewish students.

Mamma was in great spirits that year. She even enjoyed better health. Like the other mothers with whom she travelled every Saturday afternoon, she arrived with her parcel of goodies which my friends and I shared at our regular Saturday Night Ballyhoo Talent Show. This event featured extravagant dances on the cleared desktop by Mary, a girl with tiny feet whom I called Trilby, and songs by "Miss Manischewitz, the famous Matzah Soprano".

I looked forward to Mamma's visits but dreaded her questions. On the Saturday after my first practice-teaching experience Mamma asked as usual, "Nu, so what's new?"

"I suppose it's O.K." I wove between hope and reality.

"What did the Dean say?"

The dean, that towering Scotsman of whom we all stood in awe ... who, some students thought, delighted in humiliating them in the classroom ....

"The Dean?" I hesitated.

On Thursday, during my practice session in Montreal, he had popped in to find my Grade Five vigorously singing a folk song I had taught them. My conducting arm hung in the air for a moment while he strode to the back of the room, and stood there much like Hamlet's father, as I refocused myself on the children's rollicking refrain.

On Monday morning, before the assembled student body in the main lecture hall, while reviewing his visits in alphabetical order he exploded in his rich Scottish brogue.

"Miss Borrrodensky! And what werrre you doing? The place sounded like a bloomin' operrra!"

The class roared. To hear of another's frailties before hearing of one's own lessened the tension, but how was I to take his comment? Was it criticism or was it a compliment?

"The Dean says there are very few jobs," I offered Mamma the acceptable non-sequitur. "He says most of us who pass will have to take jobs in country schools." Behind this frequently repeated message lay my attempt to screen Papa and Mamma from disappointment.

One Saturday, when we had settled in for our usual talk, Mamma said, "The ladies with whom I came both say their daughters are sure they will get jobs. They're better than you?"

I shrugged my shoulders. I knew I was helping them with their projects.

As the seasons changed, we moved closer and closer to the final judgment.

Meanwhile, I was making a name for myself. I played the part of an eccentric maiden lady in the Drama Club's production of an English drawing-room comedy. I won the Prizes for Dramatics and Public Speaking. I put together a Musical for the girl who came to me for help with her project -- only to see *her* win the Hygiene Prize for writing it! Beyond belief, I was even chosen to write and deliver the Class Will at the Graduation Dinner.

When the news of job assignments finally arrived, I was one of the four Jewish girls to be placed. I trembled as I made the twenty-cent Long Distance telephone call to Mamma -- a most extraordinary indulgence.

"Mamma? Please don't faint. I'm phoning from College. I got a job!"

"What? What's wrong? Why are you telephoning?" Mamma was too excited by the Long Distance call to hear.

"I got a job, Mamma." I tried to speak calmly and distinctly.

"I'm fainting!" Mamma cried at the other end.

"Mamma, please ...! I'm telling you I got a job! To teach in Montreal. For the Protestant School Board!"

"You got a job?" Mamma whispered in utter disbelief. "But you said ... you always said ...," she repeated, not daring to utter the negative thought. "When? Where?"

"This morning. In Bancroft School. Grade Two. A letter from the Superintendent of the Board! Nine hundred and fifty dollars a year!"

"Oy, Tochter, thank you! Thank God!" Mamma got her priorities mixed. "I'll phone Papa right away. He'll be so happy!"

And so began my teaching career.

Encounters

My first year as a teacher was a very exciting year for me. There were forty-eight Jewish children in my Grade Two at Bancroft School. I relished the fresh small faces that looked to me with awe and responded to my abundant energy and creative drive with appreciation and affection. There was a new sense of anticipation and order in my life and I looked forward to each day with pleasure.

Suddenly I was a child again, a child with a mission. Through play and games I would instill in my charges the love of learning I had acquired from my parents, from teachers I had admired. I would arouse in them the curiosity which had exposed to me endless serendipities, would lead them to discoveries that made each day an adventure.

I spent endless hours decorating my classroom, inventing devices to assist the children in grasping the mysteries of words and numbers, opening new roads through literature and song, offering the wonder of making the conceptual obvious in something as intangible as 3+4 or 6x2.

Life took on meaning it had not had before. This was what I was meant to do and I did it with joy.

All my small gifts were brought into play as we dramatized story and situation, wrote and recited poetry, created sets and decorations for the various holidays.

In time, I introduced Children of Other Lands, and even as we dressed the windows for Christmas and sang the beautiful hymns and carols, I introduced the story of Chanukah and some of the songs related to that festival.

The children felt at home in the Protestant school. The parents were delighted and the principal didn't object.

Papa and Mamma were proud of me and both Mamma and Denie-Dorothy (who had grown into a tall, lovely high school student named Rusty) came on occasion to my classroom to share in my excitement and to admire the creativity of my "prodigies".

One afternoon, an errand brought me to The Main and Pine Avenue. I was about to turn the corner when I noticed her. That woman -- that older woman who was looking at me -- didn't I know her? No. It couldn't be ... Dora? Was that really Dora, the Ukrainian girl who had been in my class in Strathearn School? This heavy woman in the loose shabby coat -- the vibrant Dora?

Her large feet planted apart in dilapidated loosely-tied oxfords, she had been waiting for the light to turn green, two heavy shopping bags in her thick hands. Her mousy hair was in disarray, her teeth brown, the right central incisor missing.

As I drew near, she turned away.

"Dora!" I called almost involuntarily.

Our eyes met.

"Hello Sophie," she replied hoarsely, her breath heavy and unclean. I could see her sizing me up, my obvious prosperity in the tailored suit Papa had made for me, my leather pumps, the handsome leather handbag on my arm.

"Dora!" I began. "How are you?"

"All right," she answered softly, hardly able to meet my gaze. I recognized the eyes of her childhood, now even sadder with despair.

"You look nice, Sophie. What are you doing?"

"I'm a teacher. This is my first year. And you?"

"Me?" She smiled wearily. "I have four children ...."

I tried to control my voice. "That's a nice family," I offered. "When did you get married?"

"My modder she marry me off to an old man from her country when I leave Strattern School ...."

I was crying inside. I could hear Miss Swan's voice like a broken record, "Not all children are as lucky as you are. Not all children are ...."

"Dora," I offered my hand to my friend.

She did not take it. She looked numbly at me and as the light turned green again, she turned away.

Rite of Passage

My Bubbie's attitudes towards life and death were straightforward.

"First comes life, then comes death. God gives and God takes away. Some live long, some are not long for this world. In between, so long one lives, one must try to be a mentch."

"What's a mentch, Bubbie?" I asked, sitting beside her as she peeled potatoes in her basement kitchen.

"A mentch knows he was put here to follow the Commandments. A mentch thinks of others and tries to help those who need him. He also knows he shouldn't do to someone what he doesn't like for himself. A mentch remembers: after this world comes the Real World, the Olam ha-Emess, and we have to answer for our time here. All you can leave of yourself here is a good name."

Until the time of her death, my Bubbie carried herself straight and tall. "Tselem Elohim," she repeated, tapping me on the back to straighten up. "In His image He made us. A person has to walk straight and tall no one should have to pity him. He should live as well as he can but not tear out anyone's eyes with envy. He should always remember to look down -- so many people have less ...."

No one knew the exact date of Bubbie's birth. Nor did her children know their own birth dates. All had been inscribed in the synagogue registry in Chernobyl according to the Jewish lunar calendar. Birthdays were associated with events: six weeks after the fire in the marketplace; a month before Chaim Ber left for America; or with holidays: three days before Succot, two weeks after Chanukah. My own birthday on April 12, was remembered as eight days before Passover. When birth dates became mandatory for school in Canada, the children chose approximate dates. In this way, Bubbie's birthday was set for Purim, the Feast of Esther.

Purim. The very name evokes memories. How many Purims had we celebrated in my Bubbie's house? How many marches with my Zaida to the Shomrim Laboker Synagogue to hear the reading of the Megillah, the Book of Esther, proudly carrying our noisemakers, our graggers, which we would whirl to blot out the name of the evil Haman? Then the return to Bubbie's house for the Purim feast, to the house which rang with the voices of family and friends, the house exulting with the aroma of peppercorns, poppyseed and honey, symbols of survival, fruitfulness and a sweet life.

I, who had grown up in a secular world, envied Bubbie her gifts of piety and faith.

"One must always remember God's goodness," she said. "God has been good to me. Of the thirteen children He gave me, not counting the miscarriages, I raised ten. So many women lost most of their brood in childbed, not of us be it said .... But as the Rabbi says, 'For the very young one must not mourn. Who knows what they might have grown up to be?'

"But, why did he take my firstborn when he was already a man? Such a good man -- such a good son ...." She paused a moment, sighed, then continued stoically, "One mustn't question. No doubt I was a sinful woman ...."

I could not imagine what sins this good woman might have committed. Yet until the end of her days my Bubbie did penance, fasting on Mondays and Thursdays and allowing herself no pleasure other than those related to her family, her synagogue or a neighbour's needs.

✡ ✡ ✡

After her seventieth birthday, Bubbie said, "Now every day is a gift. All we are promised is threescore and ten." And she applied herself even more fervently to the service of those less fortunate, dropping more coins into the various alms boxes for the needy she would never see, feeding her "regulars", the poor who came for a meal on given days before the family returned from work, and to the animals who found shelter by her stove. "God's creatures," she would say. "And what are we here for?"

By her eightieth birthday, Bubbie had grown very frail. Her soft face had grown thin and wan, her gentle mouth had shrunk to a pale faint line over her toothless gums. Yet she insisted on maintaining her Monday and Thursday fasts. To her children's remonstrations and rebukes, she always had the same response. "Why? Why should I change now? God has been good to me. I'll live as long as He wants me to live -- not a day less, not a day more. The worms will have enough to eat as it is."

When the Purim of her eighty-second birthday came around, my Bubbie said, "Who knows what the morrow will bring?" And she decided to make a party.

This was another Purim. It was not in the big old house on Cadieux and Pine, the house of memory. It was in a downstairs flat on Esplanade Avenue, facing the playing fields of Mount Royal, within walking distance of the synagogue Bubbie attended when she felt strong enough to walk.

It had been a long time since the family had assembled. Surrounded by her sons and daughters and their married and unmarried children, Bubbie looked radiant despite her frailty. She wore her freshly dressed peruke and her black Sabbath dress.

The table was heavy with the remembered delicacies Bubbie made. My eye passed from the crackling Russian strudels, brown and fragrant, packed with raisins, cinnamon, nuts and homemade jams to the wispy noodle kugels leafed with apples, to the gefilte fish, white with specks of black pepper and bits of bright carrot.

"Bubbie, when did you do all this?" I asked.

"I wake so early. I can't stay in bed -- so I cooked. Come help me bring in the Purim gebeks."

My Bubbie's Purim gebeks: the yeast-blown hamantaschen (Haman-pockets) stuffed with poppyseed and honey; the taiglach, those mounds of flaky pastry morsel lightly baked, clustered with walnuts in boiling buckwheat honey; the honey-laced sesame seed squares sprinkled with ginger flaunting their allspice like incense .... As I helped her carry in the platters, all my childhood images of Queen Esther's feasts rose before me. When she brought in the enormous plaited ceremonial loaf, the Purim koilitch, and set it before the five-branched silver candelabrum, it seemed to me for a moment that the clock had been turned back to the years of my childhood again, only Zaida was no longer there to preside over this Purim feast.

Everyone brought birthday presents. When I had asked my Bubbie what she would like, she said, "I have everything I need. If you would like to give me some money, I'll give it to the synagogue. They'll know what to do with it."

I kissed Bubbie and, in Yiddish, wished her a Happy Birthday. "May you have many good years before you, Bubbie darling."

"Thank you, Donyela," she nodded wistfully. "Every day is God-granted. I only pray when the time comes He will give me a little time to prepare myself and won't let me suffer too long."

Suddenly there was a sense of separation in the air. I could not imagine there would ever be a time without Bubbie.

I looked at Papa and Mamma, at the aunties and uncles seated around the dining room. They were aging. Where were the bouncing voices of former years? I walked into the living room where the cousins and the thirty-two grandchildren, who spoke only English, were chatting politely, impersonally. The kinship which had once held the family together had become a thin filament which bound them only at bar mitzvahs, weddings and funerals. I recalled the time Papa had wanted to move our family to California because of Mamma's health and Bubbie had cried, "What? Break up the family? What else have I got?" And we had stayed. I recalled a holiday afternoon visit with Papa at Bubbie's house.

"Nobody hardly comes," she mourned.

"Everyone is busy with his own life," Papa tried to comfort her.

"It's the telephone to blame. The telephone broke up the family," she insisted. "Before, we all lived near each other -- upstairs, downstairs, around the corner, next block. In two minutes we were by each other. Now a quick ring. 'Hello Mamma.' 'Hello Shviger.' Finished. I sit alone." I knew Papa was uncomfortable. If only he could smoke, but he would not defile the day in his mother's presence.

"What can we do? It's America," he condoned. "It's America not Chernobyl. It's different times ...."

I returned to the dining room. Tea was served. The platters grew empty. People got ready to leave.

"Wait", said Bubbie. "There's a lot left. Take home for tomorrow."

"Nothing has really changed," I tried to comfort myself. "May we all celebrate your birthday again next year, Bubbie darling," I offered as I kissed her good-night.

"His will be done," she said returning my embrace. I took my package of strudel and hamantashen and went into the quiet street.

Two weeks later, Bubbie tripped in her kitchen and broke a hip. The doctor said nothing could be done for her; she must just rest in bed.

When I came to see her she was dozing. I sat by her bed in the twilight room and waited for her to open her eyes.

"How are you feeling, Bubbie?"

"Donyela, no one lives for ever. I only ask I shouldn't be a burden for long. We have a good God in heaven ...."

Bubbie lingered for two weeks weaving in and out of consciousness. The doctor came daily. The children came and went. She died in her own house, in her own bed.

I don't recall the Rabbi's words. I only recall the crowded funeral parlor on St. Urbain Street and the ten tall sons and daughters standing to have the razor blade cut into the black cloth of their clothing, the cut of Kriah, of separation from the dead, and I recall the long cortege following the hearse. Most clearly I recall the strangers, old people who pushed their way through the crowd to touch the hearse, to ask the traditional forgiveness and to beg her intercession for them in the Olam Habah, the World to Come.

"Intercede for me, Chaya-Raizl, intercede for me!" pleaded an old crone. "You were a mentch, a Tsnuah, a modest Jewish soul," she continued, keeping her hand on the slowly moving hearse, "an honest Jewish daughter ...."

"Where will I eat on Wednesday?" wailed an old beggar. "May your goodness come to greet you. You were a mentch."

A gray wind drove the leaves across the open yard of Mount Royal School on St. Urbain Street where I had attended Kindergarten. Facing it across the way, stood the synagogue where Bubbie had worshipped. As the cortege stopped for a respectful moment, I stood bonded by an ancient rite.

"Bubbie darling, intercede for me," I, the agnostic granddaughter, wept into my handkerchief. "Intercede for me, for my family, for us all ...."

Bubbie darling, with your passing, my childhood was gone forever.

Sundown --

*On the time-worn slats of the wooden bench
shadows linger*

*In the forsaken schoolyard
chalkmarks on the red brick wall
tell an indelible tale*

*In my Grandmother's old lace Sabbath shawl
designs reappear as the fabric stirs*

Afterword -- About the Author

We leave to history Bubbie and Zaida, Mamma and Papa, and Denie. Shulamis Yelin, however, went on to teach every grade from nursery to University. After Macdonald College, she studied at Sir George Williams (Concordia University), the University of Montreal and Columbia University. She married and has a daughter, Gilah -- an artist in California. Shulamis' book of poems *Seeded in Sinai* was published in 1975, and she continues to give talks, writers' workshops and readings for new readers as well as loyal fans.

Front cover photograph: Papa, Mamma, Denie (age 4) and Shulamis (age 8), 1921.

Back cover photograph: The author holding a copy of the first edition of *Shulamis*, after a reading in Montreal, 1989.

Printed by
Ateliers Graphiques Marc Veilleux Inc.
Cap-Saint-Ignace (Québec)
in November 1993